SEEING WHAT OTHERS CANNOT SEE

ALSO BY THOMAS G. WEST

Thinking like Einstein

In the Mind's Eye

SEEING
WHAT OTHERS CANNOT SEE

The Hidden Advantages of
Visual Thinkers and
Differently Wired Brains

THOMAS G. WEST

59 John Glenn Drive
Amherst, New York 14228

Published 2017 by Prometheus Books

Cover image © arosoft/Shutterstock
Cover design by Liz Mills
Cover © Prometheus Books

Inquiries should be addressed to
Prometheus Books
59 John Glenn Drive
Amherst, New York 14228
VOICE: 716–691–0133
FAX: 716–691–0137
WWW.PROMETHEUSBOOKS.COM

21 20 19 18 17   5 4 3 2 1

Library of Congress Cataloging-in-Publication Data

Names: West, Thomas G., 1943- author.
Title: Seeing what others cannot see : the hidden advantages of visual thinkers and differently
    wired brains / by Thomas G. West.
Description: Amherst, N.Y. : Prometheus Books, 2017. | Includes bibliographical references and
    index.
Identifiers: LCCN 2017006665 (print) | LCCN 2017020120 (ebook) |
    ISBN 9781633883024 (ebook) | ISBN 9781633883017 (pbk.)
Subjects: LCSH: Visualization. | Imagery (Psychology) | Creative ability. | Learning disabilities.
    | Gifted persons—Case studies.
Classification: LCC BF367 (ebook) | LCC BF367 .W47 2017 (print) | DDC 153.9—dc23
LC record available at https://lccn.loc.gov/2017006665

Printed in the United States of America

In memory of
Harold J. Morowitz, 1927–2016
Friend, Teacher, Seeker
Founding Director of the Krasnow Institute for Advanced Study
Author of many books. Coauthor of
The Origin and Nature of Life on Earth

CONTENTS

People with dyslexia are often regarded as defective, as missing something—a facility in reading or linguistic thinking—which the rest of us have. But those of us who are predominantly verbal or "lexical" thinkers could just as well be thought of as "avisuals."

—Oliver Sacks, MD

I believe those of us with Asperger's are here for a reason, and we have much to offer.

—John Elder Robison

Dyslexia is Britain's secret weapon in the spy war: Top code breakers can crack complex problems. . . . Most people only get to see the jigsaw picture when it's nearly finished while the dyslexic cryptographists can see what the jigsaw looks like with just two pieces.

—GCHQ official

During residency, I recognized that I had dyslexia. And then I realized I had this gift for imaging. Radiology is where I belonged. I live in a world of patterns and images and I see things that no one else sees. Anomalies jump out at me like a neon sign. . . . I do have a gift that other people don't have, and I will always stay ahead of the crowd and see more in an image than other people.

—Beryl Benacerraf, MD

Many of the most exciting new attempts to apply deep learning are in the medical realm. . . . While a radiologist might see thousands of images in his life, a computer can be shown millions. . . . "This image problem could be solved better by computers . . . just because they can plow through so much more data than a human could ever do." The most remarkable thing about neural nets is that no human being has programmed a computer to perform any of [these] stunts. . . . In fact, no human being could. Programmers have, rather, fed the computer a learning algorithm, exposed it to terabytes of data—hundreds of thousands of images or years' worth of speech samples—to train it, and have allowed the computer to figure out for itself how to recognize the desired objects. . . . In short, such computers can now teach themselves.

—Roger Parloff

PREFACE

Scholars and artists thrown together are annoyed at the
puzzle of where they differ. Both work from knowledge; but I suspect they differ most importantly in the
way their knowledge is come by. Scholars get theirs
with conscientious thoroughness along projected lines
of logic; poets theirs cavalierly and as it happens in and
out of books. They stick to nothing deliberately, but let
what will stick to them like burrs where they walk in the
fields. . . . The artist must value himself as he snatches a
thing from some previous order . . . where it was organic.
. . . There must have been the greatest freedom of the
material to move about in it and establish relations in
it regardless of time and space, previous relation, and
everything but affinity.

— Robert Frost, "The Figure a Poem Makes,"
essay in *Complete Poems*

In a brief essay, the poet Robert Frost provides us with an important
insight about how we learn and how we know. It is remarkable how his
observations cut across whole volumes of psychology and give us two different ways of looking at our world. And his words explain to me how my
own mind works and provide me with an explanation of what I am trying
to do with this book.

My first book, *In the Mind's Eye*, was modeled on the methods of
the scholar. It is the product of years of research in the Library of Con-

gress and the National Library of Medicine. Like a detective, I followed the stories and questions wherever they took me. Guided by my intellectual mentors, Norman Geschwind and Samuel Torrey Orton, and others like them, I tried to understand the fundamentals of the science and the history of the original observations, the changing perceptions and definitions, the evolving concepts. And I tried to build a persuasive point of view quoting the most respected authorities—trying to understand the distinctive talents and capabilities of dyslexics and strong visual thinkers.

By looking so far and so broad, I often found material and quotations that fit my perspectives and arguments better than I could have ever imagined. If I had tried to create or invent these quotations, I could never have done better. The perfect statement or observation was just sitting there, waiting to be found.

I have always worked as an outsider, without specialist training or an official professional position to explain or defend, to shape my perspectives. Yet, at the same time, I have also been an insider. I am a dyslexic visual thinker and come from a family of artists and engineers—including some dyslexics, mild or strong, and some perhaps with traits linked to Asperger's syndrome.

Based on my personal experience, I always had a strong sense of what was relevant and who was to be believed. I wandered through the literature and listened to what people said at the conferences. I learned much from the rich, century-long history of observations and investigations from the literature, from the old timers, and from the passionate advocates. I even learned from the jokes, such as: "Never trust a surgeon who can spell." I think that my first book is still very much alive after all these years because of the insights and stories I slowly uncovered during those years of broad searching. (No PhD committee would ever have allowed me to do what I did.) But I think it was worth the effort.

However, I want this new book to be different. Combining the old with the new, looking beyond dyslexia to a range of different thinkers, I want to begin to understand how and why some people "see what others cannot see." I claim no final insights. But I want to begin the process by sharing these stories. With this new book, I want to follow the way of the poet, as described by Frost. During the twenty-five years since my first book was published, I have traveled often, given many talks, and met a great many extraordinary people. I have walked through many fields. Much has stuck with me—mostly without intention—but much has proved to be worth retelling. With brief stories and without complex references or argument, I now want to share some of what I have learned.

Thomas G. West
Washington, DC

INTRODUCTION

Since *In the Mind's Eye* was first published in 1991, I have had the privilege of providing presentations for many different kinds of organizations in the United States and in nineteen other countries. In the process, I have met and learned from, people whom I consider some of the smartest, most creative and most interesting people on the planet. Many of them are dyslexic or, as it is described these days, "on the spectrum," with Asperger's syndrome or other learning differences. Still others are merely very strong visual thinkers—people who habitually think in pictures (and who may have trouble with words or numbers).

With this book, I will draw together some of the observations and stories that I have accumulated since *In the Mind's Eye*'s publication. As I mentioned in the preface, in that book, I took a scholarly approach with a great many references and notes to support my perspectives and arguments. I am taking a very different approach with *Seeing What Others Cannot See*. Here I will be focusing on brevity and simplicity—using a collection of short stories and excerpts, layering a worldview with minimal explanation and discussion.

I hope that these stories and observations will help others to begin to see how important these visually oriented capabilities are for high-level work in many fields—and how little they are understood and appreciated in traditional education and in conventional measures of intelligence and ability. I make no claim to special knowledge or expert status. I just want to share with visual thinkers and different thinkers what I have learned, in the hope that it will help them along the way—and in the hope that it will influence the direction of future research and practice.

Some forward-looking organizations have come to appreciate and value these visual capabilities, but most educators and employers seem to be stuck in old ways of thinking. (The psychologists say, "We have got it covered—with our well-established 'performance' tests." Artists, designers and visually oriented scientists respond, "No, you have not even begun to see what we see.")

Over centuries, we have built an academic system that relies mainly on words and numbers. However, we are now living at a time when powerful visualization technologies, together with emerging large-scale problems, are driving us toward a new realization of how much we need to develop a new kind of thinking—and how much we need the kinds of people and the kinds of brains that have been marginalized in the past by the dominant specialist culture, mostly based on proficiency with words rather than images.

In the last few decades, the world has changed in important ways. And it is changing once again. We need to understand current trends and not be blinded by traditional beliefs and practices. When we take the long view, the trend lines appear to be quite obvious. But many professionals and experts are well trained to see and believe what they were taught decades ago. In a time of major change, it is vitally important to listen to people who can see what others cannot see.

When traveling with my first book, I would talk with scientists, physicians, designers, artists, inventors, and others. They often made the remark that their dyslexic colleagues had a different way of looking at things and "could see things that others could not see"—whether in reference to an indefinite ultrasound or x-ray image, or regarding a novel surgical procedure or the solution to an enduring scientific puzzle. At first, I came to believe that this capability was most often characteristic of those dyslexics who were also strong visual thinkers.

Later, I was surprised to hear the very same words used by an advocate talking to a group of high school students with Asperger's syndrome. In the same vein, another advocate had written and discussed with me her own propensity to think in pictures—seeing things in her work that others did not notice or think were important. Indeed, she had asked one researcher and writer, "How do you think at all if you don't see pictures in your mind?"

Over the years, I heard similar observations hundreds of times, in hundreds of different places. Gradually, I came to realize that I was dealing with a pattern of consequence, one that many had observed in a variety of different fields. The cumulative effect was that I was handed an intriguing topic—and a book title—that I could no longer ignore.

It is apparent that visual thinkers seem to experience the world differently from nonvisual individuals and other "neurotypicals." And this, I believe, is a good thing—although it is not usually recognized as such, especially in the early years of education. I have learned that for some people, the easy things in primary school can be quite hard—while the hard things in graduate school and in advanced work situations can be quite easy.

Over time, I have come to realize that I have had the considerable advantage of gaining a special perspective into remarkable parts of our world—providing me with distinctive insights into diverse and alternative ways of thinking, learning, and working—all related, apparently, to observing things in a deeply original and perceptive manner.

It is often noted that some dyslexic scientists or entrepreneurs need only a brief mention of an idea or concept. They don't need to read the rest of the report. They just think about it, and all of the implications and future problems and potentials become immediately apparent. They do not need a painful elaboration of the obvious (or, rather, what is obvious to them but not necessarily so with neurotypicals).

As always, I have continued to rely mainly on stories, or anecdotes, and first-person accounts. I have come to trust them more than I do the many conventional academic theories and studies based on large-scale surveys. I listen to what the affected individuals tell me. I believe that they know what they are talking about. They live it every day. And I believe that it is important to look at a whole individual life story to see how mixed strengths and weaknesses manifest themselves through time in changing economic and social circumstances. You can assemble the data and count the frequencies later; but you first must look at the individual life story, like a good medical history, to see the most important overall patterns. If you are mainly looking at many people, using the established conventional tests, you may be measuring and counting the wrong things.

When you look, as an outsider, at a century or two of evolving conventional thinking, you can see how often the winds have changed or have blown the wrong way. In hindsight, it is often easy to see who was on the right track from the beginning—and how long it has taken for the conventionally trained experts to abandon outdated beliefs.

These observations are especially true in regard to the different thinkers we focus on here. In a way, it is self-evident. If you see what others do not see or cannot see—most will say that you are wrong or, in some way, a heretic. It is not pleasant for the conventional experts to see threatened the material that they have been teaching for many years—or to have their books and articles suddenly become outdated or irrelevant. It is always so.

These stories and first-person accounts have provided me with a set of primary sources that permit me to gain insights perhaps rarely otherwise available—and I hope these will be of interest to everyone. This approach is not unlike the style of the late Oliver Sacks—who kindly provided a foreword and blurb for the second edition of *In the Mind's Eye*.

Over these years, I have also been fortunate to meet a number of individuals who were eager to tell me their own life stories. Indeed, several individuals who have been at the very top of their fields—including, for example, one of the leading individuals in the early development of modern molecular biology—as well as a major figure in the emerging specialist field of pediatric surgery. Both of these individuals contacted me after reading my first book—saying, in one way or another: "I read your book. You understand how I think. Others do not. I want to tell you my story."

I have been surprised at the remarkable range of fields and occupations of those who have shown interest in these topics—including scientific, medical, art, design, computer, and entrepreneurial business groups. In many cases, attendees and contacts have shared with me observations that were, apparently, not generally known—and sometimes well hidden.

In time, I found that these observations seemed to fit into a larger pattern, acknowledging the value of diverse minds and diverse brains—especially when this diversity is beginning to be highly valued in a time of rapid technological change and global economic competition. We are becoming more aware that we need something other than the conventional clerks or strong test takers or traditional narrow specialists—although our educational system continues to train and select them.

Instead, I believe that our very survival may depend on strong visual thinkers and practically minded visionaries, those who think in different ways, those who see the larger patterns, those who seem to be able to see over the horizon and predict what is coming, and those who naturally think in moving pictures by mental manipulation of three-dimensional shapes and forms—increasingly aided by the newest integrative graphical computer technologies.

Remarkably, I have continued to be surprised at the serious interest in these perspectives among the most highly successful individuals. These individuals seem to immediately understand that high creativity and capabilities are often linked to visual thinking or to dyslexia, to Asperger's syndrome or other learning differences. In general, strangely, it seems that

Nobel Prize winners are highly interested in these perspectives—whereas there appears to be very little interest among most teachers, school psychologists, and educational administrators. They might find much more talent among their students if they knew how and where to look for it.

In many respects, Asperger's syndrome (which I regard as still a useful term although some professional groups have recently discontinued its use) appears to be the complete opposite of developmental dyslexia. However, many individuals in both groups appear to share a strongly visual manner of thinking, a link that is not always obvious but could be extraordinarily important—especially in an era when high-level work in many fields increasingly involves "scientific visualization" and visual analysis of complex information.

In addition to these powerful trends, it appears that, historically, many of the most creative and productive in regards to technological innovation and scientific discovery have been strong visual thinkers. In contrast, it appears that many nonvisual thinkers may be very good at learning and applying old knowledge (and doing well on exams, often getting the top grades and the top jobs) but may be very poor at creating new knowledge or developing the broad and deep understanding so badly needed for modern, real-world challenges. What spelled success in the old specialist culture may very well generate major failures in the new.

In *Seeing What Others Cannot See*, I want to focus mainly on visual thinking—and its considerable power in many different fields to understand relationships and novel solutions not often available in other ways. Among computer graphics folks, words and numbers are seen as the "thin pipe to the brain." In contrast, they see computer graphics and information visualization as "the fat pipe to the brain." I hope that this book will begin to illuminate what the "fat pipe" can do—and how it is changing the fundamentals of our world.

Mostly, I will be looking at some of what I have learned in retrospect—

but I hope to look a little way forward as well. As we know, for years computers and automation have been taking over low-level jobs. In more recent years, the newest and most powerful computers and machines have played into the hands of visually oriented different thinkers—providing powerful tools well suited to their mix of talents and special abilities.

However, the context is changing once again. Now in the early days of "deep learning," we can expect shortly to see major effects on very high-level jobs as well. The machines are now learning to see patterns that only high-level, experienced professionals could see before. In some cases, they have already surpassed human capabilities. It has long been expected. But after several false starts, it appears that the time has arrived. The effects are not yet entirely clear, but it is likely that these trends may require the distinctive talents of "different thinkers" once again. Then we will badly need to listen to those who can see what others cannot see.

Chapter One

SEEING THE WHOLE

What this analysis showed was that Mars had almost nothing but carbon dioxide. Just bare traces of other gases were present. And I knew immediately that this meant that Mars was probably lifeless. And at that moment, suddenly a thought came into my mind. But why is the Earth's atmosphere so amazingly different?

—James Lovelock

LOOKING FOR LIFE ON MARS— UNDERSTANDING LIFE ON EARTH

In September 1965, the British scientist James Lovelock was asked by NASA to help with the design of ways to determine whether there was life on Mars. He met with other scientists, mostly biologists, to discuss the design of instruments and detectors that could be transported to Mars— which was then thought to be somewhat similar to the Mojave Desert. So they talked of soil types and landing craft. One scientist even built a tiny metal cage for the fleas that might be found on the animals that might be living in the Mars desert. Lovelock said this approach made no sense to him since we could not know if life on Mars would be in any way similar to life on Earth. The director of the scientific group was not happy and challenged Lovelock to come up with a better idea—"by Friday."

Under time pressure, Lovelock had a "Eureka moment" evoking an idea that had not occurred to him before. He thought one had to only analyze the gases in the atmosphere of Mars (from a distance) to see whether life was there. He thought that, if life were there, the organisms would have to use gases from the atmosphere to help build their bodies, and they would have to give off their waste gases to the atmosphere as well. He happened to be working in the group with the astronomer Carl Sagan—who, with an associate, used data from a special telescope to analyze from Earth the gases of Mars. They found that almost the whole Mars atmosphere was nothing but carbon dioxide—with only a few traces of other gases. Accordingly, Lovelock considered that there was probably no life on Mars after all.[1]

However, in rapid fashion, Lovelock started to ask himself—if this is true for Mars, how does this work on Earth? Initially, Sagan did not like Lovelock's idea. But then Sagan noted a long-standing scientific puzzle: Over billions of years, our sun has increased in power by 30 percent—yet Earth has remained habitable for life. If Earth was warm enough for life long ago, how are we not now "boiling"? Lovelock asked himself, how was this possible? How could Earth continue to be cool enough for life even when the sun was growing so hot? How was Earth different from Mars? Could it be that living things on Earth were somehow regulating the gases on the planet—and this, in turn, was regulating the temperature of the planet as well?

In this way, the idea of a self-regulating Earth was born—now known as Lovelock's "Gaia hypothesis" or later "Gaia theory." As other scientists have noted, this leap required an unusual kind of mind—one capable of seeing Earth from the "top down" as a whole, not just from the perspective of one scientific discipline or another. Because of his rather unconventional career, Lovelock was famous for having knowledge and experience in many different disciples, as well as experience with hands-on instrument invention. He was perhaps more able than most to integrate the various parts of the puzzle.

In the BBC documentary *Beautiful Mind: James Lovelock*, in which he tells this story, Lovelock also says, "it so happens that I am dyslexic, but not seriously."[2] He says the dyslexia slows him down on exams and causes confusion in handling certain mathematical equations. We may well wonder to what extent Lovelock's dyslexia (and the kinds of thinking that seem often to go along with it) would have helped him to see the really big picture and, as a consequence, see what others could not see, forever altering the way we all see our whole planet.

«»

Looking at the life story of James Lovelock, one can hardly imagine anyone who fits better the kind of pattern that we are focusing on in this book. Over and over again he has seen what others could not see or would not see. As one scientist observed, "[Lovelock's] mind is able to make intuitive leaps or connections in things that the rest of us would always keep separate in our heads and it is these connections that he has been able to see that he has gifted us."[3]

Lovelock has always been independent and unorthodox, certainly not a specialist. And he was clearly, by his own account, dyslexic, although as we noted, "not seriously." He has described his father's reading problems. Like James, his father was also an inventor and tinkerer, and he had a great knowledge of the world of nature. Now we have some evidence for at least two generations of these traits.

Lovelock is the author of a number of books, but mostly not about himself. However, fortunately, we have now access to several interviews and some very well done documentaries on his life and on his distinctive approach to science. Indeed, one documentary by the BBC in the series *Great Minds* (quoted above) is so well put together, with material so well selected, that one could write a small essay on almost every one of Lovelock's assertions and stories. It is quite remarkable.

Lovelock has had recognition for many inventions and discoveries. Chief among these are the electron capture detector and the Gaia hypothesis. The electron capture detector is extremely sensitive. Some say that the sensitivity of this detector allowed the careful measurements of small amounts of chemicals in the atmosphere. The detector is thus credited with helping to start the green movement with concern about the CFCs (chlorofluorocarbons) in the atmosphere and the well-known "ozone hole." Two scientists, not Lovelock, received the Nobel Prize for their work with CFCs and the ozone hole. But all of their attention was based on data originally collected by Lovelock using his own invention.

Originally these data were collected mainly because Lovelock was personally curious about the new haze that he had seen over the woodlands where he used to walk with his father. This was a change. He saw that CFCs were a "people marker." He found that they had spread all over the planet, and they did not degrade. Fortunately, the problem could be addressed by stopping production by a few companies. Lovelock notes that dealing with "global heating" is not so simple or easy.

As everyone knows, the controversies about climate change and global warning are endless. However, cool minds continue to shed light on this hot topic. Referring to a very recent book by Anthony McMichael, *Climate Change and the Health of Nations*, reviewer Anita Makri summarizes the author's position and recommendations:

> Scepticism, doubt, and denial don't escape McMichael's attention. He argues that not believing in climate change originates from a human tendency to favor urgent, survival-enhancing reactions over responding to gradual changes. Can the brainpower we evolved in times of climatic

stability be channeled toward changing the behavior that undermines this stability? he asks. McMichael concedes that change is not easy. He focuses on motivating action by speaking to the public about climate change not in the abstract but in terms that are closer to home, akin to everyday experience. Through education and informed discussion, let's talk of debilitating heat, not emissions; parched crops, not scenarios. . . . This way, he says, there may be a chance to activate the "fight or flight" response that befits this threat to our survival.[4]

VISUAL THINKERS AND VISUAL DISCOVERIES

For centuries, those who think visually and those who think differently have struggled at the edge of a world of education and work mostly dominated by those who think in words and numbers instead of images and mental models. It is not often fully appreciated how much these two groups represent cultures that are vastly different—different in ways of working and different in ways of thinking.

Visual thinkers and different thinkers like Lovelock have long been, apparently, among the most creative and innovative in the sciences as well as in art, design, and other fields. In recent decades, the rapid rise of information-rich computer graphic data and information visualizations—coupled with new global economic challenges and easy access to massive data sources—has turned the conventional world of information upside down, although few with conventional "expert" knowledge have yet noticed. (Sociologists and psychologists have just begun to realize that their conventional studies of twenty subject individuals seem like nothing when compared to social media, which can easily and rapidly survey thousands or millions.)

It seems clear that recent educational reforms (and more recent reforms of the reforms) in the United States and elsewhere have merely reinforced the long-standing conventional values and methods, leading to "teaching to the test," along with almost universal boredom and widespread fear, while the visual and other creative talents (actually the most valuable talents in this new visual-digital world) are misunderstood and ignored.

More recently, as visual thinkers and other different thinkers aided by these new technologies increasingly move toward center stage, it is hoped that their capabilities will come to be recognized and fully valued—and that these thinkers will be in a better position to formulate actions based on big-picture solutions to big-picture problems.

The growing awareness of the value of visual-spatial talent is a topic I have been dealing with explicitly as a researcher and writer for over twenty-five years; yet in many ways, I now realize, it has been a topic that I have been thinking about for most of my life. Coming from a family of artists and engineers, silversmiths, and millwrights, and at least one movie stunt pilot, I have always recognized the value of thinking in pictures and the value of precision motion in 3-D space.

But in the early days, my great puzzle always was how to bring visual talents to bear on conventional school subjects, especially in the early years. Visual talents are so often not understood or are misunderstood. The usual formal academic approaches did not seem to be appropriate. I finally settled on the notion that what would be most useful to readers would be to describe a more personal story—with a series of examples, as one problem and one discovery led to another series of observations and insights—those that in time resulted in my two earlier books, *In the Mind's Eye* and *Thinking like Einstein*.

VISUAL THINKING: AMAZING SHORTCOMINGS, AMAZING GIFTS

During my historical research, I had learned about how visual thinking and visual-spatial talents (together with varied learning difficulties) seemed often to be associated with major scientific discoveries of the past. However, I did not have to look long for current examples of major scientific discoveries. As sometimes happens, the examples and stories came to me—as in the case of the molecular biologist Bill Dreyer, who, in an interview, explained:

> I knew I was different in the way that I thought, but I didn't realize why I was so dumb at spelling . . . and rote memory and arithmetic. . . . The first time I realized how different . . . brains could be . . . was when I bumped into Jim Olds at a dinner party back in the late sixties. Jim . . . was a professor here [at Caltech] . . . famous for his pleasure center work. . . . A speaker talked about the way we think and compared it to holography. Jim was across the table from me. I said, "Oh, yes. When I'm inventing an instrument or whatever, I see it in my head and I rotate it and try it out and move the gears. If it doesn't work, I rebuild it in my head." And he looked at me and said, "I don't see a thing in my head with my eyes closed." We spent the rest of the evening . . . trying to figure out how two professors—both obviously gifted people at Caltech in the Biology Division—could possibly think at all, because we were so different. So then I took this up with Roger Sperry [Nobel laureate and near laboratory neighbor], and I realized that I had some amazing shortcomings as well as some amazing gifts.

The passage above is excerpted from the oral history project at the California Institute of Technology in Pasadena.[5] The speaker is the late William J. Dreyer, PhD, who has been increasingly recognized as one of the major innovators in the early days of the biotech revolution that is now washing over all of us. In September 2007, one of his inventions was placed in the National Museum of Health and Medicine in Washington, DC—the first gas-phase automated protein sequencer, which he patented in 1977. The sign over the machine on exhibit reads: "The Automated Gas-Phase Protein Sequencer: William J. Dreyer and the Creation of a New Technology."

A strong visual thinker and dyslexic, Dreyer developed new ways of thinking about molecular biology. With his powerful visual imagination, he could somehow see the molecules interacting with each other. Sometimes he was almost entirely alone. He (with his colleague J. Claude Bennett) advanced new ideas based on new data about how genes recombine themselves to create the immune system.

These ideas turned out to be twelve years ahead of their time—well ahead of everyone else in this emerging field. Most did not like this new theory because it conflicted with the conventional beliefs held by most experts in the field at the time. "It was so counter to the dogma of the time that nobody believed it," his widow, Janet Dreyer, explained to me.[6] William Dreyer's approach also used a form of scientific investigation ("peptide mapping") with which most immunologists were then unfamiliar. "Knowing what we know now, pretty much any biologist would look at Bill's data and say that is what it has to mean. But few could understand it then," Janet noted. However, gradually, they all learned to think the way Dreyer thought. Then, it was obvious that Dreyer (and Bennett) had to be right.

TO SEE WHAT OTHERS CANNOT SEE

In his earlier school days, Dreyer had the usual difficulties experienced by dyslexics who are also very bright. But in time, in college and graduate school, he began to find roles that made use of his strengths—while he learned to get help in his areas of weakness. He joined a study group. The others in the group all took careful notes in the lectures. He took no notes. He just sat there while he listened and observed carefully. Then, after the lecture, his fellow students provided him with the detailed data, and he told them what it all meant. "He was giving the big picture and all the major concepts," explained Janet Dreyer. Eventually, surviving a major life-threatening illness made William Dreyer realize that it was time to refocus his life—and then his fascination with the laboratory work began to draw him in.

Soon, the young Bill Dreyer became a star in the laboratory. While in graduate school in Seattle, Washington, and while working at the National Institutes of Health (NIH) in Bethesda, Maryland, he could tell his professors and colleagues which were the best experiments to do. Somehow he knew how to proceed and where to go in this brand-new field of study that later came to be known as protein chemistry. His professors and section heads would write the grants, get the funding, and write the papers for him, based on his ideas and observations. "The money just came. Because he was doing good work, grants would just be there for him," observed his widow. He was happy at NIH but eventually (after a previous Caltech offer had been refused) in 1963 Caltech persuaded Dreyer to come to Pasadena as a full professor at the age of thirty-three. Clearly, the value of his pioneering work had been recognized.

Later, however, because of the further development of his then heretical ideas, William Dreyer could not get funding from academic or foundation sources for inventing and building his new instruments. Furthermore, his department head would get irate phone calls from professors from other institutions complaining about Dreyer's publications and talks. Dreyer gave many talks at the time that made some attendees angry, although others could see the importance of his innovative observations.

"He was on the lecture circuit then and he [gave these talks] a lot." Of course, these were not really unproven theories, explained Janet. She pointed out that Dreyer was sure of his ground because he had the data to prove the veracity of his ideas. "It was not merely a hypothesis in that paper; it was real data." However, it was data in a form so new and so alien that almost everyone in the field could not understand what he was talking about. Much later, these professors, and all their students, came to see that William Dreyer had been right all along.

Because he could not get funding from the usual sources, Dreyer went to private companies to manufacture his instruments; this was quite unusual and discouraged at the time, but it is now wildly popular among universities hoping for a share of large royalty payments. Seeing the potential for his inventions (and their scientific impact) but having a hatred of administration and corporate politics, Dreyer came to be, as he told me, the "idea man" for seven new biotech companies (including Applied Biosystems), and he bought himself a high-altitude, pressurized, small airplane with some of the proceeds.

Years later, in 1987, Susumu Tonegawa was awarded a Nobel Prize in Physiology or Medicine for work he had done in Switzerland. His innovative sequencing work proved (through experiments that were illegal in the United States at the time) that Dreyer and his colleague had been correct in their predictions many years earlier.[7]

LEARNING BY DOING—JUST IN TIME

Later in his life, Dreyer taught molecular biology to his dyslexic grandson, Brandon King, who was clever with computers but was having a very hard time in high school. Employing King as a kind of apprentice, Dreyer would start each workday (using a form of applied just-in-time learning) saying something like: "I want you to write this little Internet search program for me today but first let me explain the biology you need to know to do this task." In time, working with Dreyer, King skipped the latter part of high school, most of college, and all of graduate school and was doing advanced "post-doc" level work—writing computer programs and doing advanced programming developing databases, graphic user interfaces (GUIs), and other tools. King also used sophisticated scientific information visualization techniques to help link various human traits to sections of the genetic code.[8]

In doing this work, Dreyer's grandson notes that he uses his "visual thinking ability to design the architecture of the programs . . . visualizing the components in his head, trying it out and fixing what doesn't work, before I write the code—much like my grandfather. . . ." He was not only doing high-level work; some argued that King was in fact working at the leading edge—in later years co-authoring peer-reviewed journal articles.[9] Indeed, one of King's work colleagues only obtained his own doctoral degree (and a required publication) because King was able to write a tutorial and GUI that helped a member of the colleague's required publication review committee to better understand the significance of the advanced work done by the colleague.

Bill Dreyer, who was never one to read many books, did read *In the Mind's Eye*. He telephoned me to explain his reaction to the material: "Your book describes the way I think. This is my life. The next time you come to LA area, let's talk. I want to tell you my story."[10] This contact led to many visits, many discussions, some recorded conversations, and a long-term friendship. Dreyer died of cancer in the spring of 2004. One of the enduring passions of his later work had been to try to understand the relationship between visual thinking, dyslexia, and the high levels of creativity he had experienced in his own life and work. He had participated in a small conference on visualization technologies and dyslexia held at the National Library of Medicine in Bethesda, Maryland, flying east with Janet in his own plane.[11]

Years afterward, as his health declined, Janet eventually sent out news to friends that he had stopped eating and was nearing the end. I read the e-mail at an Internet cafe in Dublin, Ireland, where I had been giving talks for the Irish Dyslexia Association. I immediately phoned Bill from our hotel, and to my surprise we had a long conversation, our last. Shortly afterward, I traveled back home to Washington, DC, and then on to Pasadena, arriving the day before he died. He was then unable to talk, but I assured him that I would continue the work that he thought so important. My second book, *Thinking like Einstein*, is dedicated as follows, to "William J. Dreyer, 1928–2004, molecular biologist, strong visual thinker, prescient inventor, instrument maker, who loved to fly high to see what others could not see, frequently alone."

MAGNIFICENTLY ILL-ADAPTED ENGINES OF DISCOVERY

The story of the life of William Dreyer and his grandson, Brandon King, brings into sharp focus the considerable advantages, in the right setting, of the visual thinking, dyslexic kind of brain—at least of certain variations within the great diversity of dyslexic brains. (Of course, this story also strongly suggests what sometimes might be possible when employing nontraditional educational approaches such as apprenticeship or home-schooling.) We can see that this kind of brain—seemingly so magnificently ill-adapted to conventional education at all levels—can be a powerful engine of insight, innovation, and discovery.

This kind of brain may cause many problems in early schooling but it may also, sometimes, raise some individuals rapidly to the top of some new field of knowledge—pushing forward way beyond the many who had been conventionally successful students but who find it hard to conceive of anything really new or really important. Perhaps they cannot see through to the novel, unexpected solution because they have learned too well exactly what the teacher wanted them to learn, what was expected on the conventional test. They cannot easily unlearn what they have been taught.

(One high-achieving researcher at NIH, with three professional degrees, in law, medicine, and pharmacology, once admitted to me—to my amazement—that he was aware of his own limitations, that he was constrained beneath a kind of glass ceiling. He was aware that in spite of all his academic accomplishments, he "was not dyslexic enough" to do the kind of really original, creative, and important work he had seen in his dyslexic colleagues.[12])

With stories such as these, we can begin to understand that these visual-thinking dyslexics do indeed see the world differently. They think differently. They are not like nonvisual, non-dyslexics. They are not like each other. Often, they seem to "see things that others do not see." (It was during these years that I first noticed how this same phrase—with almost exactly the same words—was repeated with striking frequency in many different and unconnected settings.) Yet these same individuals have great difficulty with things that are easy for almost everyone else—especially at the lower levels of education. In schools, they are constantly tested on what they are not good at—almost by definition. No one seems to be interested in what they *can* do. Everyone is most concerned with what they *can't* do.

Why are they never tested, we should ask, in the areas where they have enormous talent and can make major contributions in their later life and work? Can teachers and school psychologists believe that this is feasible? I hope that some of the stories offered here will create a new vision of what is possible. But this new vision will almost certainly require the development of new tests and measures, ones quite different from conventional academic measures but perhaps that are better suited to the new realities of life and work—better suited for the visual-thinking dyslexics but also better suited for many non-dyslexics as well.[13]

RICHARD FEYNMAN AS VISUAL THINKER

I often attended the August computer graphics conferences held at the Convention Center in downtown Los Angeles. During these visits, I would also spend time with Bill Dreyer at Caltech or at his home in Pasadena. Bill would tell me about his latest research work. Sometimes he would tell me with excitement, for example, about how he tapped into certain journal articles on the Web and was able to see patterns in the data or photographs that the article authors had not seen.

Other times he would talk about how he was able to quickly identify the strong visual thinkers from among the faculty at Caltech and other universities. Bill felt that he could tell a lot about a person from just a short conversation. His discussions with the nonvisual scientist Jim Olds (quoted above) were typical. Dreyer told me that he thought there were only a few highly visual professors Caltech—but they were often among the most creative and innovative.

One of Dreyer's favorites among the visual thinkers was his old personal friend Richard Feynman. He had known Feynman for many years—indeed, he told me that they rented the same beach house in Mexico in the summers, in alternate months. As Bill suggested, of the strong visual thinkers, Feynman is an especially interesting one who provided a number of valuable insights. Feynman's ways of working and thinking offered a wonderful contrast to the more conventional scholars and scientists.

ANYTHING IN THE UNIVERSE

James Gleick's book about Richard Feynman, *Genius*, provides several delightful and illuminating portraits. In the passage quoted below, we have a classic illustration of the battle between two very different ways of thinking about a problem—ways that converge on the same solution, although from different directions (more or less).

> Julian Schwinger's quantum electrodynamics and Richard Feynman's may have been mathematically the same, but one was conservative and the other revolutionary. One extended an existing line of thought. The other broke with the past decisively enough to mystify its intended audience. One represented an ending: a mathematical style doomed to be fatally over-complex. The other, for those willing to follow Feynman into a new style of visualization, served as a beginning. Feynman's style was risky, even megalomaniacal.[14]

According to Gleick, Schwinger and other physicists were trying to extend the conventional mathematical approaches—the known concepts and techniques—just a little bit further. They wanted an incremental improvement. On the other hand, Feynman, not unlike the stereotypical "visionary," wanted a great deal more. He "was searching for general principles that would be flexible enough so that he could adapt them to anything in the universe."[15]

Time and time again, Feynman provides us with wonderful examples of the working and thinking style of the strong visual thinker—and how different this is from that of colleagues and competitors who follow the more conventional verbal, logical, and mathematical approaches—approaches that have dominated many scientific fields. These stories can provide us with insights that extend in many directions.

Where others used mainly mathematics, Feynman (like Albert Einstein, James Clerk Maxwell, and Michael Faraday—as we will see in the next chapter) relied heavily on diagrams, pictures, and mental models. Indeed, Feynman once told an associate: "Einstein's great work had sprung from physical intuition and that when Einstein stopped creating it was because 'he stopped thinking in concrete physical images and became a manipulator of equations.'"[16]

MERE DEFINITIONS

Just as Feynman's style of thinking was in deep contrast to Schwinger's, so too it was in most respects entirely different from another important physicist, Murray Gell-Mann. As Gleick observes, "In so many ways these two scientific icons had come to seem like polar opposites. . . . Gell-Mann loved to know things' names and to pronounce them correctly. . . . Feynman . . . despised nomenclature of all kinds. Gell-Mann was an enthusiastic bird watcher; . . . Feynman's [belief] was that the name of a bird did not matter. . . ."[17] Repeatedly, we see Feynman making the point that simply naming a thing does not demonstrate that you really understand it in any meaningful way—a fundamental idea that is in opposition to basic education and testing at all levels, often especially in the sciences. (He was furious that his own young children were being taught not real science, as he saw it, but "mere definitions."[18])

Gleick cites comparisons of the visual Feynman and the verbal Gell-Mann at some length: "Physicists kept finding new ways to describe the contrast between them. Murray makes sure you know what an extraordinary person he is, they would say, while Dick is not a person at all but a more advanced life-form pretending to be human to spare your feelings."[19] Murray was interested in many things but was "openly contemptuous" of branches of science outside high-energy physics. In contrast, "Dick considered all science to be his territory—his responsibility—but remained brashly ignorant of everything else."[20]

Their use of the body is important. "Feynman talked with his hands—with his whole body, in fact—whereas Gell-Mann, as [one] physicist and science writer . . . observed, 'sits calmly behind his desk . . . hands folded, never lifting them to make a gesture. . . . Information is exchanged by words and numbers, not by hands or pictures.'" The power of these brief descriptions of very different styles of thinking should not be underestimated. "'Their personal styles spill over into their theoretical work, too. Gell-Mann insists on mathematical rigor in all his work, often at the expense of comprehensibility. . . . Where Gell-Mann disdains vague, heuristic models that might only point the way toward a true solution, Feynman revels in them. He believes that a certain amount of imprecision and ambiguity is essential to communication.'"[21]

With all their differences, however, each man is passionate in the honesty and directness with which they approach their subject. "Gell-Mann was no more likely than Feynman to hide behind formalism or to use mathematics as a stand-in for physical understanding."[22] Yet both men projected masks to the world that became important parts of their personal realities. "'Murray's mask was a man of great culture. . . . Dick's mask was Mr. Natural—just a little boy from the country that could see through things the city slickers can't.'"[23]

VISUAL AND MUSCULAR TYPE

It is important for us to note that for Feynman, and others like him, what was needed was not only or entirely visual. It was something just beyond the visual—as it extends naturally into the physical. These kinds of thinkers needed "a kind of seeing and feeling" grounded in "physical intuition." We should note again here that Albert Einstein made similar observations. Einstein pointed out that in his own thought processes, part of his "vague play" with "signs and more or less clear images" were "elements" that were "of visual and some of muscular type."[24] Clearly, for some, there seems to a close association between moving images in the mind and moving muscles and parts of the body.

As Gleick observed, "intuition was not just visual but auditory and kinesthetic. Those who watched Feynman in moments of intense concentration came away with a strong, even disturbing sense of the physicality of the process, as though his brain did not stop with the grey matter but extended through every muscle in his body. A Cornell dormitory neighbor opened Feynman's door to find him rolling about on the floor beside his bed as he worked on a problem. When he was not rolling about, he was at least murmuring rhythmically or drumming with his fingers. In part, *the process of scientific visualization is a process of putting oneself in nature: in an imagined beam of light, in a relativistic electron. . . .*"[25]

Feynman tried to explain how his approach was not entirely or exclusively visual. As he was quoted in *Genius*, "What I am really trying to do is bring birth to clarity, which is really a half-assedly thought-out pictorial semi-vision thing. I would see the jiggle-jiggle-jiggle or the wiggle of the path. . . ."[26] Gleick notes that "in seeking to analyze his own way of visualizing the unvisualizable [Feynman] had learned an odd lesson. The mathematical symbols he used every day had become entangled with his physical sensations of motion, pressure, acceleration. . . ."[27] "When I start describing the magnetic field moving through space," Feynman observed, "I speak of . . . fields and wave my arms and you may imagine that I can see them. I'll tell you what I see. I see some kind of vague, shadowy, wiggling lines . . . and perhaps some of the lines have arrows on them—an arrow here or there which disappears when I look too closely. . . . I have a terrible confusion between the symbols I use to describe the objects and the objects themselves."[28]

INHERITING THE EARTH—USING THE FAT PIPE

The contrast between Feynman and Gell-Mann vividly conveys the difference between how they think and work. If the world is shifting, as I believe, toward the visual, what can we expect? What will be learned? How will it be taught? What talents and proficiencies will be valued more—and which less?

Quietly, the previously (largely) powerless visual minority seems now to be moving into position to master the newest and most powerful technologies—while the old guard hardly understands what is happening—instinctively resisting substantial change. Within modern institutions, with many conventional verbal thinkers, there is still almost no awareness of the usefulness of the new image-based technologies, which every year grow increasingly powerful and more pervasive. "Give me," they say, "the text or the tables of numbers. Why would I want to use pictures, diagrams, or computer visualizations? Pictures are for children."

Computer graphics workers have long observed that computer images are the "fat pipe" to the eye and the brain. Words and numbers need only a "thin pipe" and little computer power. Images and simulations, on the other hand, require massive computer power—power only widely available in recent years. Also, to be most effective, these new image technologies require a receiving brain that can handle the massive and complex data that the images represent—that is, the kind of brain that cannot stop itself from thinking mainly in complex images instead of a stream of words.

The increasing awareness of the value and power of visual thinking has many consequences. Now, in the second decade of the twenty-first century, most of us have on our desks (or even in our pockets) the power of what was only available in early supercomputers. But most of us have no idea how to use this power. Already we are putting this power in the service of genuinely new forms of education and work.

Some of us feel a new sense of urgency. We have powerful new tools. But we now have a much bigger job than ever before. All of our students and workers need to be much better educated to compete in a global marketplace. So all of us need to find and develop areas of strength using the widest range of tools and methods available—not just traditional academic skills. It seems clear that the traditional courses and assessment methods will no longer do the job. There must be many different paths to many forms of success and productivity.

The use of visual methods and technologies are providing an important path for a broad range of students, at all education levels, to doing high-level work. Many surprises should be expected along the way. Some of the students at the bottom of the class in the old system (based mainly on words and reading) are already at the top of the class in the new system (based mostly on information-rich graphics and images)—although few professionals understand this.

I have been observing and writing about the development of these technologies for more than two decades. And I have come to believe that their impact could be more important than the development of the movable-type printing press centuries ago. The problem is to deeply rethink what our students need to learn in this new century and how we can guide them—helping them to develop their own visual talents and to learn to see what others do not or cannot see.

THE NEW ECONOMY

Even just over the lifetime of today's students, many of the basic clerical skills that have long dominated education at all levels have already become less important in an economy and marketplace where these tasks will be increasingly taken over by semi-intelligent machines. With these changes, we should expect that the visual-spatial talents, big-picture thinking, manipulation of mental models, pattern recognition, and creative problem solving will become increasingly important in the workplace, as greater use is made of computer graphics, visualization techniques, and interactive multisensory technologies to understand and communicate information about complex systems and discontinuous trends.

In the long view, ideas of ability and talent in the workplace are conditional and depend on the context of the times. After decades of rapid change in many areas but remarkable continuity in others, it now appears that we are going through a period of major change—turning upside down conventional ideas of what is worth doing, what is worth learning, and who is considered intelligent. In many cases, the kinds of education that prepared our generation and our parents' generation for work and life are being seen as entirely unsuitable for our children and our students.

A REPEATING CYCLE—NOW WITH "DEEP LEARNING"

Nearly seventy years ago, Norbert Weiner in his book *Cybernetics* (he invented the word) predicted a sequence of events that we all see unfolding all around us today. Accordingly, he set forth the context in which we might usefully think about education and work in a rapidly changing world economy. According to Weiner, we are seeing a repeating cycle. In the 1800s, muscle power was taken over by machines and no one could make a living wage in competition with the new machines.

Similarly, as we are seeing now, those with basic clerical skills or even those with pedestrian academic, managerial, or professional skills may find it increasingly difficult to find buyers for their services in the marketplace. More recently, of course, this situation is exacerbated as Internet technologies open the global marketplace to new forms of direct global competition.

We know that machines have replaced assembly line workers and bank tellers, and we may not be surprised to see an erosion of opportunities for those with certain manual or clerical skills. However, many of us still may not be ready to adjust our fundamental thinking based on unprecedented changes in many managerial and professional roles.

And in recent months, we are seeing how "deep learning" in computing coupled with massive data availability is beginning to compete successfully with very high-level professional skills in medicine and elsewhere. In the past, the professionals may have based their expert judgments and experience on many thousands of images—whereas these new machines can rapidly, and cheaply, survey many millions of images to accurately detect a cancer or some other disease pattern.[29]

Weiner, as one of the fathers of computing and control systems, saw it all coming long ago. Writing from the National Institute of Cardiology in Mexico City in 1947, he explained: "Perhaps I may clarify the historical background of the present situation if I say that the first industrial revolution, the revolution of the 'dark satanic mills,' was the devaluation of the human arm by the competition of machinery." Once this form of competition was in place, there would be "no rate of pay at which a . . . pick-and-shovel laborer can live which [would be] low enough to compete with the work of a steam shovel. . . ."[30]

In the next phase, which is now ever more rapidly unfolding all around us, "the modern industrial revolution is similarly bound to devalue the human brain, at least in its simpler and more routine decisions."[31] There are likely to be some exceptions: "Of course, just as the skilled carpenter, the skilled mechanic, the skilled dressmaker have in some degree survived the first industrial revolution, so the skilled scientist and the skilled administrator may survive the second." However, the overall trend is clear: ". . . Taking the second revolution as accomplished, the average human being of mediocre attainments or less has nothing to sell [that] is worth anyone's money to buy." We can easily see the prescience of Weiner's somber observations, as machines have increased in power by many orders of magnitude since his day—and as his second revolution moves closer to fulfillment with increasing rapidity. We now know that many of the most routine functions of the copy editor, the bank clerk, and the bookkeeper are being done more rapidly and more cheaply by machines. In similar fashion, we are now seeing the rapid expansion of a formerly less expected trend: computer systems learning to reliably replicate the professional judgments of attorneys, engineers, accountants, architects, physicians, and investment bankers.

Referring to the work of economist Paul Krugman, the *Economist* observed some time ago: "Lawyers and Accountants . . . could be today's counterparts of early-19th-century weavers, whose incomes soared after the mechanisation of spinning only to crash when the technological revolution [finally] reached their own craft."[32] Shortly, we may be seeing an almost exactly similar situation, as "deep learning" threatens to replace the expert work of many high-level professionals, from radiologists to architects to lawyers.

In the nearly seven decades since Weiner's appraisal, much has come about that was unexpected, but the basic form and direction of this relentless and accelerating trend has remained unchanged. It has become increasingly clear that not only clerical and other "low-level" functions are subject to threat—but also, in time, many functions and jobs are threatened that formerly were thought to require high intelligence and advanced degrees.

These changes should force us to rethink the fundamentals of education and work, as the rules of the game are changing in dramatic and unexpected ways. We will all need to adjust our ideas of talent and intelligence. And, in this world turned upside down, we may expect that some, or perhaps, many of the students who are at the bottom of the class in the old word-dominated system will rise to the top of the class in a new world where the real work will involve the high-level thinking that will involve the recognition and manipulation of complex information presented in visual-spatial patterns. Here we can expect that many of the visually proficient dyslexics and different thinkers to thrive.

WORD BOUND

Written language is a technology—a powerful technology, but still a technology. In the long history of human survival, technologies change—and some in-born traits may help or hinder proficiency in the particular technologies dominant at one time or another. As technologies change, the kind of brain that lends itself poorly to an old technology may be just what is wanted with a new technology.

Reading and writing are adaptations to a particular technology. Strong visual thinkers and dyslexics have long been plagued with the mismatch of their abilities to the requirements of education and employment—the requirements of this particular technology. Sometimes, one who is surprisingly slow with certain verbal tasks—making them appear to be of low intelligence—may be strikingly fast and proficient in certain high-level, visual-spatial, nonverbal tasks. For some, this pattern has long been recognized. But for many others—schooled to assume, deep down, that intelligence is unitary (and largely verbal)—this is a new and revolutionary idea.

It is remarkable to see how many very well-educated people can be totally unaware of the one-sidedness of their views on verbal intelligence. They commonly argue, for example, that it is impossible to think clearly without words. Of course, those who make such statements often work in heavily word-bound occupations. However, much also depends on the culture of the workplace. In some organizations, there must be endless written memoranda before anything can be done.

In others, most communication is oral and is oriented to action; memos are never written. Still, many assume that one is not intelligent if one does not use words skillfully and often—a frequent assumption especially in academic circles. However, when it comes to a really successful design or strategy or the forward-looking decision that allows an organization to survive and prosper, the skill of writing may be seen as unimportant or irrelevant.

The importance of visual talent is acknowledged by psychologist Howard Gardner. Although he argues for several forms of intelligence, he readily recognizes a special status for visual-spatial intelligence in contrast to verbal intelligence. "In the view of many, spatial intelligence is the 'other intelligence'—the one that should be arrayed against, and be considered equal in importance to, 'linguistic intelligence.' . . . For most of the tasks used by experimental psychologists, linguistic and spatial intelligences provide the principle sources of storage and solution."[33]

A NEW BALANCE

I am not trying, of course, to underrate the value of the written word. Its power is obvious and pervasive in literature, politics, religion, history, science—indeed, almost every sphere of knowledge—and in every means of transmitting knowledge across the generations. Its power is so great, however, that many have been in danger of believing that it is all that there is. Most of our institutions are built around it. The role of language will always be extremely important, whether written or recorded or transmitted in some other manner.

The case I am trying to make, however, is that the new visual technologies will promote a greater balance between words and images—involving a gradual shift to using nonverbal capacities in doing high-level and high-value work. With these changes, the words will be used to comment, to point out, to discuss. But the real center and core of the work—the real application of talent—will be in understanding the images, not the words. If my expectations are correct, those who wish to do this kind of high-level work will need to be as comfortable with images as they are with words. They will no longer be allowed to work in the one-sided manner that is now commonplace in many fields.

Appearances can be deceiving. For example, a storyteller was once asked how it was possible to remember all the words for his many traditional stories. His reply was that he never remembered any words, as such. Rather, he saw the story like a movie in his mind's eye—and merely related in words what he saw in images.[34] This process is entirely different from a memorized text.

Accordingly, we may argue that the old system of education and work has paid too much attention to the words alone—partly because they are so powerful, are so cheap, and fit so easily the dominant technology of paper, printing, reading, and books. However, with the new visualization technologies and techniques, we might expect to find that the process of rendering ideas visually may be made sufficiently rapid and inexpensive to allow a shift toward a boarder use of this additional mode of communication—permitting more of us to understand and communicate concepts about areas of life and thought that do not lend themselves readily to the world of words alone.

Many professionals who deal with academic learning difficulties or dyslexia or other learning differences assume that career options are limited for these populations in a world long dominated by words. They start with the assumption that the main task is to remediate areas of weakness to come up to the minimum standard required in a word-oriented world. They rarely look for nonverbal strengths—and they almost never focus on the development of these strengths. In contrast, we might expect that the current direction of technological change will progressively favor the talents that many strong visual thinkers have, while their difficulties are likely to become less and less important over time.

There was a time when skill in reading and writing was relatively unimportant—for farmers, sailors, ship builders, mothers, weavers, merchants, warriors, craftsmen, and kings. Now we assume that the need for conventional literacy is almost universal. However, we may soon need to consider the growing need for a new form of "visual literacy."

It may not be long before visualization technologies and techniques spread into many areas that formally were thought to be the exclusive domain of words alone. Thus, in this new, more balanced world, we might expect a higher regard for a range of abilities—and a higher regard for the needed contributions of people who are unusually good with images, although they may have trouble with words.

NEW TECHNOLOGIES TO SEE WHAT OTHERS DO NOT SEE

Seeing differently. Seeing the unseen. Understanding patterns with incomplete information. Comprehending the complex whole. Seeing things that others do not see or cannot see. In the past, some of the most original scientific thinkers have used their own special powers of imagination and visualization to build mental models in their mind. Eventually, these insights were converted to words and mathematical formulas so that they could be communicated to others. In most cases, however, it seems that the greatest interest has been in the resulting formulas that could then be memorized and tested—rarely is there interest in the visual modes of thought employed to arrive at these formulas in the first place. However, all of this has begun to change. A number of trends in several fields are converging to revive long-dormant visual approaches.

During the past few years, with the development of these new tools and techniques associated with graphic computers, the methods previously accessible to only a few highly gifted individuals (in their own imagination) are becoming available to much larger sectors of the less gifted population. What only a few highly visual thinkers could see in their mind's eye now can been seen by many on the screens of these increasingly powerful and comparatively inexpensive machines.

Over the years, various research centers have been stimulated by the development of sophisticated graphics capabilities and "scientific visualization." According to one observer, "with the advent of graphics, researchers can convert entire fields of variables . . . into color images."[35] With these new techniques, "the information conveyed to the researcher undergoes a quantitative change, because it brings the eye-brain system, with its great pattern-recognition capabilities, into play in a way that is impossible with purely numeric data."

FROM LECTURES TO SIMULATORS

Increasingly, the power of visual approaches is coming to be appreciated in many fields. However, at the same time, some are becoming aware of the curious fact observed by neurologists that great visual talents do seem to come at some cost; that is, those who have very high visual talents sometimes seem to have corresponding areas of weakness, often in verbal areas.

Current developments in technology and in the workplace are expected to transform the way we think of talent and capability such that those who seem to be poorly fitted for an old-fashioned world of traditional subjects and memorized texts may be remarkably well suited for the coming world of technological change and complex visualization. Most notably, we might expect that among the newly appreciated areas of talent will be the brain's ability to use new computer graphic and data visualization technologies to recognize patterns and invent creative and innovative solutions to problems—using mainly visual-spatial capacities rather than memorized, rule-based analytical instructions. Accordingly, one can argue that the skills and talents that will be seen as most important in the coming decades will be those that are most difficult for a machine to replicate—that is, creative and inventive pattern recognition and complex problem solving employing visual and spatial capabilities.

With these changes, past evaluations of desirable talents and skills could be changed as well, gradually but dramatically. Of course, the conventional verbal, clerical, and managerial skills will always be needed and valued to some extent, but these will not be considered as important or as useful in themselves as they were previously. Before too long, we may find that semi-intelligent machines will be more "learned" and better read, with more complete and accurate memories, than even the most experienced and most conscientious of the traditional scholars and experts in any field.

In the near future, consequently, instead of the qualities desired in a well-trained clerk or traditional scholar, we might find it far more valuable to develop the qualities associated with visual thinkers such as Leonardo da Vinci: a facility with visual-spatial perspectives and modes of thought instead of mainly verbal (or symbolic) fluency; a propensity to invention by making connections among many diverse fields; an ability to learn directly through experience (or computer-simulated experience) rather than primarily from lectures and books; a habit of continuous investigation in many different areas of study; and the more integrated approach of the global thinker rather than the traditional narrow specialist; an ability to move quickly through many phases of research, development, and design using mental models and imagination, incorporating modern three-dimensional, computer-aided design systems.[36]

Thus, it seems that we might be in a position to come full circle, using the most advanced technologies and techniques to draw on some of the most old-fashioned human capacities. We can simulate reality by computer rather than describing it in words or numbers. Students can now learn, once again, by doing rather than by reading or listening to lectures. They can learn, once again, by seeing and experimenting rather than by following memorized texts, rules, and algorithms. In so doing, all of us will learn greater respect for the nonverbal abilities and intelligences that were always vitally important but have been generally eclipsed by a disproportionate emphasis on the verbal abilities most valued by traditional teachers and professors in the higher-prestige academic tradition. Sometimes, the oldest pathways and most primitive capacities can be the best guides into unexplored new territory.

REVERSALS IN THE WORKPLACE

After centuries of comparative continuity, there is now a need for fundamental change. In recent decades, the prestige of the verbal academic approach was largely overwhelmed the long tradition of multisensory, hands-on learning. Perhaps, we will now see an unexpected movement back the other way. We might move forward by seeming to move backward. For today's students and workers, many of the basic verbal and clerical skills that have long dominated education at all levels will cease to be as important as they once were. In the new economy, these tasks will be increasingly taken over by semi-intelligent machines, as predicted by Norbert Weiner long ago.

In this new economy and marketplace, the visual-spatial talents, global thinking, pattern recognition, and creative problem solving are now becoming increasingly important. The recognition of this trend will accelerate as greater use is made of data visualization, computer graphics, and interactive multisensory technologies to understand complex systems and predict unexpected trends.

Many companies and employers will find that in order to survive they will need to adjust to new categories of thought and new rules of practice. In a similar fashion, educators will need to adapt to new realities, as they try to free themselves from an almost universal preoccupation with written symbols, the instruments of the old technology. Accordingly, as we all struggle to adapt ourselves to deep changes in thinking and working, some strong visual thinkers will doubtless play once again their oft-repeated role. We should expect to find them working creatively at the edge of the new frontier, reading little but learning much, experimenting, innovating, establishing a new path forward—learning from direct experience, anticipating where things are going, and seeing what others do not see.

Chapter Two

VISUAL PERSPECTIVES

Albert Einstein, twenty-six years old, published in the
Annalen der Physic in 1905 five papers on entirely different subjects. Three of them were among the greatest
in the history of physics. One, very simple, gave the
quantum explanation of the photoelectric effect—it was
the work for which, sixteen years later, he was awarded
the Nobel Prize. Another dealt with the phenomenon
of Brownian motion, the apparently erratic movement
of tiny particles suspended in a liquid. . . . The third
paper was the special theory of relativity, which quietly
amalgamated space, time, and matter into one fundamental unity. This last paper contains no references and
quotes no authority. All of them are written in a style
unlike any other theoretical physicist's. They contain
very little mathematics. . . . The conclusions, the bizarre
conclusions, emerge as though with the greatest of ease;
the reasoning is unbreakable. It looks as though he
had reached the conclusions by pure thought unaided,
without listening to the opinions of others. To a surprisingly large extent, that is precisely what he had done.

—C. P. Snow, *Einstein: A Centenary Volume*

> [Visual thinkers have] often seemed to be in the
> minority—although they seemed to be part of an espe-
> cially creative and productive minority.
>
> —Howard Gardner, *Frames of Mind*

SOLITARY MEALS WITH EINSTEIN

For me, the turning point in my story is clear enough—my solitary meals in a grand hotel in Cairo in the summer of 1986. I was working for an international engineering and consulting company and we were managing a large-scale energy project with the Egyptian Electricity Authority funded by USAID. The project director was on vacation, so I was doing his job in Cairo for three weeks while he was away. The hotel was full of mothers and children from Saudi Arabia, wanting to escape the greater heat of Riyadh. The young boys tried to play soccer in the patch of green around the swimming pool. I appeared to be the only Westerner in the entire hotel. I spent my mealtimes reading books about Albert Einstein, especially his own *Autobiographical Notes*, the slender volume in which he explains how his thinking had been shaped from boyhood on.

I had always been fascinated by Einstein—at once almost universally acknowledged as the genius of our age—but also known to be eccentric and to have had trouble in his early schooling and career. I did not know it at the time, but he was to become my main guide throughout my research—introducing me to his own heroes and intellectual mentors—especially James Clerk Maxwell and Michael Faraday. These were names I knew only vaguely. But as I learned more, I saw that these three shared great respect and an extraordinary intellectual rapport across time—largely because they all relied heavily on their visual-spatial talents as the source of their remarkably original (and enduring) insights and discoveries.

Over time, these considerations became the core of my research as I dug through primary sources such as letters and diaries, with one insight leading to another as I reviewed a period of nearly two centuries. I found unfolding a distinctive pattern of thought, innovation, and discovery—one that was useful to a small group long ago—but one that has become ever more pervasive over recent years with the advent of new technologies along with new discoveries in physics, biology, mathematics, and other fields. Visual thinking—once so productive for a few—was now becoming more important for the many—partly because of new approaches to science and mathematics—and partly because of increasingly powerful new tools and technologies.

VISUAL TALENTS AND VERBAL DIFFICULTIES

There is increasing evidence that many highly original and productive thinkers have clearly preferred visual over verbal modes of thought for many tasks. Some argue that visual-spatial abilities should in fact be seen as a special form of intelligence on par with verbal or logical-mathematical forms of intelligence.[1] Historically, it is apparent that some of the most original and gifted thinkers in the physical sciences, engineering, mathematics, and other areas relied heavily on visual modes of thought, employing images instead of words or numbers. However, it is notable that some of these same gifted thinkers have shown evidence of a striking range of learning problems, including difficulties with reading, spelling, writing, calculation, speaking, and memory. What is of greatest interest here is not the difficulties themselves but their frequent and varied association with high visual and spatial talents.

Some researchers believe that sometimes high visual talents are closely associated with various kinds of learning difficulties because of certain early patterns of neurological development. They have argued that in some forms of early brain growth, the development of the verbal left hemisphere is suppressed while the development of the visual right hemisphere is increased—producing an unusual symmetry of brain form and function.[2] In ordinary people, they have argued, sections of the left hemisphere tend to be larger than in the right. However, in visual thinkers with verbal difficulties, the left and right hemispheres tend to be of similar size. Varied visual talents mixed with verbal difficulties are evident in a diverse group of highly gifted historical persons: Michael Faraday, James Clerk Maxwell, Albert Einstein, Henri Poincaré, Thomas Edison, Leonardo da Vinci, Winston S. Churchill, Gen. George S. Patton, and William Butler Yeats.[3]

MICHAEL FARADAY

I found it instructive to follow Einstein's lead and learn more about Michael Faraday. An English scientist of the early 1800s, Faraday was the son of an unemployed blacksmith. He was for years a welfare recipient and had very little formal education. However, after eight years as an apprentice bookbinder—with a Frenchman who had fled to London to escape the French Revolution—he started work as a bottle washer and junior laboratory assistant. Through years of self-education and intensive laboratory work, he eventually became director of the laboratory, the Royal Institution, and earned a reputation for being the greatest experimental scientist of his time—formulating, among many accomplishments, in chemistry and physics, the basic ideas of electricity and magnetism. Faraday started with chemistry and moved on to physics and the study of electricity, light, and magnetism. He thought of himself as a "philosopher" and hated being called a "chemist" or a "physicist" because he hated the limited worldview of the specialist approach. He liked to look at wholes, not pieces.

Among many original discoveries, he developed the first electric motor. But most important, he developed utterly original ideas about the fundamental nature of energy and matter—the electromagnetic "field" and "lines of force." These ideas were later translated into proper mathematical form by James Clerk Maxwell and still later became an important influence on the young Albert Einstein. Remarkably, these ideas have proved to be valid and useful since the time they were first developed in the middle of the nineteenth century. With each new scientific revolution since then, many old theories and concepts have become rapidly outdated; but on the whole, those of Faraday and Maxwell just keep looking better and better.[4]

As a youth, Faraday explained that he was not precocious or a deep thinker. But he said that he was a "lively imaginative person"[5] and could believe in the Arabian Nights as easily as he could the encyclopedia. However, he found a refuge from this too-lively imagination in experimentation. Known especially as a great experimenter, he found he could trust an experiment to check the truth of his ideas as well as to educate and inform his intuition, his mental models. In the experiment, he said, he "had got hold of an anchor" and he "clung fast to it."[6] Finally, Faraday is seen by later scientists as being like Einstein in that he had a remarkable ability to get to the heart of the matter and not be distracted by details or blind alleys. Historians of science say that Faraday "smells the truth."[7] They think he had an "unfailing intuition," and they wonder at "his inconceivable instinct."

JAMES CLERK MAXWELL

Maxwell was the sort of scientist who was able to deal in an extraordinary way with two entirely different worlds—the world of conventional mathematics and analysis, and the visual world of images and models and diagrams—the latter of which he, along with Faraday, favored. Indeed, he understood and admired Faraday's visualizations as did no other scientist of their time. Eventually, he converted Faraday's ideas into mathematics, which are now known as "Maxwell's equations," although he always maintained that these were originally Faraday's ideas.[8]

A native of Scotland, James Clerk Maxwell received his education in science and mathematics at Cambridge University in England. He showed himself to be a brilliant student. However, Maxwell's troubles with words manifested itself in severe, lifelong speech problems. He was a stutterer and had continuous career difficulties as a result—although he is thought to be the most brilliant physicist of the nineteenth century. In fact, Richard Feynman said in 1963 that "from the long view of the history of mankind—seen from, say, ten thousand years from now—there can be little doubt that the most significant event of the nineteenth century will be judged as Maxwell's discovery of the laws of electrodynamics."[9] "The American Civil War," Feynman said, "will pale into provincial insignificance in comparison with this important scientific event of the same decade."

Like Faraday, Maxwell was a strong visual thinker. In the biographies and letters as well as the commentaries of historians of science, there are many references to this proclivity of Maxwell. He could understand Faraday's highly visual ideas much better than others could, presumably because his visualization abilities were as exceptional as Faraday's were. He was familiar with the mathematics required—as Faraday was not— and was able to translate the conceptual clarity of Faraday's theories into the language of mathematics. He much preferred Faraday's conceptions to those of the other professional mathematicians of his day. Indeed, he felt that following Faraday's way of looking at things produced a conceptual clarity and simplicity impossible through the other more acceptable scientific approaches of their time. Further, in an extraordinary observation Maxwell notes that it was a good thing that Faraday knew no mathematics—because if he had, he could easily have been diverted from his best insights because of the conventions of mathematical thought.[10]

Maxwell's visual orientation was evident in many aspects of his work (although he avoided this approach when he needed to). In mathematics and physical science, his starting point was often geometry. He used mechanical analogies and resorted to diagrams and pictures whenever possible. Much of his work involved the interaction of force and substance in a largely visual-spatial arena. And, finally, one historian of science, writing of Maxwell, puzzled at the appearance of artists in his family, generation after generation, although the family seemed to be otherwise a uniformly practical group.[11]

ALBERT EINSTEIN

In the life of Albert Einstein, the importance of visual learning and visual talents in conjunction with verbal difficulties has long been recognized. His poor memory for words and texts made him hate the rote learning methods of his early school years. However, he tended to thrive later at the progressive school in Switzerland, where he prepared to take his university examinations—no doubt, partly because the unconventional school was based largely on visually oriented educational principles.[12]

There is a debate among biographers and scholars as to whether the young Einstein was a brilliant student or whether he was a dullard. After some time looking at these conflicting points of view, I realized that to some extent he was both—a pattern that is typical of highly gifted visual thinkers with verbal difficulties. Einstein's sister, Maja, recorded a number of details about his early life, commenting about his late development of speech; his slow answers but deep understanding in mathematics; and his frequent calculation errors even though he had a clear understanding of the main mathematical concepts involved.[13]

In secondary school, he dropped out of school in Germany (contrary to plan) to follow his parents after they moved to Italy. His reason was that because of his "poor memory," he preferred to endure all kinds of punishments rather than to have to learn to "gabble by rote."[14] After he failed his first set of university entrance examinations, Einstein went to a new and unconventional school—one that was based on the highly visually oriented educational ideas of Johann Heinrich Pestalozzi. It was at this school that Einstein's abilities began to blossom and the great theories later published in 1905 began to take their initial shape.[15]

The coexistence in Einstein of visual talents along with verbal difficulties has been noted by several observers. Suggesting the recognition of a general pattern, the physicist and historian of science Gerald Holton has remarked:

> An apparent defect in a particular person may merely indicate an imbalance of our normal expectations. A noted deficiency should alert us to look for a proficiency of a different kind in the exceptional person. The late use of language in childhood, the difficulty in learning foreign languages may indicate a polarization or displacement in some of the skill from the verbal to another area. That other, enhanced area is without a doubt, in Einstein's case an extraordinary kind of visual imagery that penetrates his very thought processes.[16]

Later, in his own writing, Einstein made clear references to what he saw as two very different modes of thought, especially with regard to his own most creative and productive work. He pointed out that when he did really productive thinking, he always used "more or less clear images" and what he called "combinatory play," as the "essential feature" in his "productive thought," as well as of some "visual and some muscular type."[17] But he explains that if he wanted to communicate these thoughts to others, he had to go through a difficult and laborious translation process, proceeding from images to words and numbers that could be understood by others.

It is anticipated that modern visualization technologies and techniques may eventually permit many more ordinary people to do what Einstein did with mental models in his mind's eye—and permit the communication of sophisticated visual ideas without having to resort to poorly suited verbal and mathematical substitutes.

The great power of the visual approach is underscored in one rather surprising account of Albert Einstein's development as a professional scientist. In his later career, Einstein did become increasingly sophisticated in higher mathematics. However, some have argued that this increased sophistication may have been more of a hindrance than a help in his later creative work. The mathematician David Hilbert made clear, with some exaggeration, that Einstein's creative scientific accomplishments came from elsewhere than through his mathematical skill: "Every boy in the streets of Gottingen understands more about four-dimensional geometry than Einstein. Yet, in spite of that, Einstein did the work and not the mathematicians."[18]

Hilbert was not alone. Indeed, Abraham Pais, the author of a scientific biography of Einstein, observes that Einstein's increasing reliance on mathematics over time also involved a reduced dependency on the visual methods that he used so heavily and so productively in his earlier work. Pais suggested that this change in approach may have contributed to Einstein's comparatively reduced productivity in his later years. Pais observes:

"It is true that the theoretical physicist who has no sense of mathematical elegance, beauty and simplicity is lost in some essential way. At the same time it is dangerous and can be fatal to rely exclusively on formal arguments. It is a danger from which Einstein himself did not escape in his later years. The emphasis on mathematics is so different from the way the young Einstein used to proceed."[19]

THINKING LIKE EINSTEIN ON THE *HOKULE'A*

We have Hawaiian names for the houses of the stars—the places where they come out of the ocean and go back into the ocean. If you can identify the stars, and if you have memorized where they come up and go down, you can find your direction. The star compass is also used to read the flight path of birds and the direction of waves. It does everything. It is a mental construct to help you memorize what you need to know to navigate. . . .

We use the best clues that we have. We use the sun when it is low on the horizon. . . . When the sun gets too high you cannot tell where it has risen. You have to use other clues. Sunrise is the most important part of the day. At sunrise you start to look at the shape of the ocean—the character of the sea. You memorize where the wind is coming from. The wind generates the swells. You determine the direction of the swells, and when the sun gets too high, you steer by them. And then at sunset we repeat the observations. . . . At night we use the stars. . . .

When I came back from my first voyage as a student

navigator from Tahiti to Hawai'i the night before he went home, [my teacher] . . . said "I am very proud of my student. You have done well for yourself and your people." He was very happy that he was going home. He said, "Everything you need to see is in the ocean but it will take you twenty more years to see it." That was after I had just sailed 7,000 miles.

—Navigator Nainoa Thompson of the
Polynesian Voyaging Society, on having sailed
on the traditional Polynesian canoe, the *Hokule'a*.

Using the Best Cues We Have

With the words of navigator Nainoa Thompson, in this passage we see a wonderful description of using well the best of what is ready at hand to do a most important job—on which rests the survival of a whole people.

Indeed, during recent years, the successful voyages of the Hokule'a and other long-distance canoes have become cultural milestones, and Nainoa Thompson has become a major hero among Polynesians. These voyages and revived navigation skills have much to teach us all. We are shown a highly refined example of the observation and visual thinking skills needed to navigate across the Pacific. If we had not known better, most of us would have thought that it was not possible to navigate accurately this expansive ocean without the aid of modern technology.

Perhaps we are just now mature enough in our modern culture to fully appreciate what these navigators accomplished in an earlier culture with the simplest of tools and the most sophisticated use of their brains—and to see that such feats rank with the highest accomplishments of human beings, in any field, at any time.

We can now see that it is not a matter of developing complex mathematics or the most modern tools and technologies. Rather, it is a matter of using well what is available in the particular situation—developing techniques to train the brain and the senses through close observation, long practice, and sensitive teaching—making the best use of what is at hand, using "the best clues that we have," as Thompson put it.

Feats such as these draw heavily on visual and spatial abilities and "intelligences" that have been generally underappreciated in modern culture. But all of this is changing, and the newest technologies are taking us back to some of our oldest and most essential abilities—teaching us that in some fields, the further forward we proceed, the more we reconnect with our ancient roots.[20]

Thinking Visually—Thinking like Einstein

Visual thinking and visual knowledge—these are a continuing puzzle. They seem to come up more and more these days—but few seem to understand their deep roots and larger implications. The human brain is indeed wonderful—the way it permits us to use all forms of natural systems and subtle information to do rather unbelievable things—and still survive, or, rather, in the long run, in order to survive.

To navigate across thousands of miles of open ocean while feeling the long-distance swells (not sailing past tiny unseen islands just over the horizon), to adapt to amazing extremes of heat and cold—using with great sophistication only those tools and resources that are readily at hand—all without modern technologies or distant supports and hidden subsidies (always a major advantage for modern travelers) . . . all of this is accomplished without a book of written instructions. And without full scientific knowledge, but with knowledge well suited to hunt food, find home, build shelter, fend off enemies, cooperate with a group, and raise a family—for thousands and thousands of years.

Strangely, the farther ahead we go, the more our future is seen to be like our distant past. Sometimes, the more we look into our future, the more it is like the very, very old. The more modern we become, really, the more we come to appreciate (belatedly) the long-earned wisdom of traditional cultures.

The more we understand the brain's deep resources for creativity and pattern recognition, the more we come to respect the accomplishments of our distant ancestors—and appreciate the problems they solved—the solutions that have secured our survival and allowed us to be. The more we move into unfamiliar territory, without map or guidebook, the more we admire traditional knowledge long discounted by bookish education.

This is not mere romanticism but levelheaded respect. The more our technologies change (and also change us), the more we can see that the newest computer data visualization technologies draw on some our oldest neurological resources, more like those of the hunter-gathers than they are like those of the scribes, schoolmen, and scholars of more recent times. Albert Einstein tells us, as we have seen previously, that all of his truly important and productive thinking was done by playing with images in his head, in his imagination. Only in a secondary stage did he translate—with great effort, he says—these images to words and mathematics that could be understood by others. We now have technologies that can deal with the images directly—so the laborious translation may often not be necessary or even desirable.

THE RISE OF VISUAL TECHNOLOGIES

Some believe that visualization technologies are already in evidence everywhere. They think the battle is over. Others, myself among them, think that visualization technologies have a very, very long way to go, and they have hardly begun to have substantial impact in the full range of fields that they will transform over time. I think, with the exception of a few specialists, the process of deep change has not yet really begun. Indeed, I think that gaining insight and new understanding through the sophisticated use of visualization technologies and techniques, in time, should be as pervasive as reading and writing.

But there can be little debate that we already have tools that can help us think the way Einstein thought—and it is striking how old and traditional these ways of thinking were. In many ways, Einstein thought and worked more like a craftsman than a scholar. And, indeed, the more proficient he became at the sophisticated science and mathematics of his peers, as we have noted, the less visual he became—and, much more important, the less creative and innovative he became.

It would seem that the traditional Polynesian navigators were drawing on some of the same neurological resources that were so very useful to Einstein when he was a young man—before, as we are told by other scientists, he became corrupted by excessive familiarity with sophisticated mathematics. As he became more expert as a scientist and mathematician, he accomplished less. He had abandoned the visual modes of thought that had given him his best and most original insights.

TRADITIONAL VISUAL CULTURES

When I was giving talks to teachers and school heads in Fairbanks, Alaska, some years ago, I was told that the Athabaskan Indian students in the villages along the Yukon River were natural visual thinkers and natural scientists. This should make us think.

We may well wonder whether they would have substantial advantages if they were to be educated in the visual world of Einstein's imagination and modern computer graphics—rather than the old academic world of facts and dates, words and numbers. Shortly afterward, when I was giving talks in Honolulu, others there told me that traditional Polynesian culture quite naturally promotes highly visual and hands-on approaches over verbal approaches to the communication of knowledge.

If we were to fully and deeply understand the roots of knowledge in our own new world, we might see that Einstein's way of thinking is far more like those used in resurrected traditional cultures than it is like the academic conventions of the past. We might see, again, that Einstein's way of thinking is more like that of the artisan or craftsman or traditional navigator and less like that of the conventionally trained scholar or mathematician or scientist.

Chapter Three

SEEING ALONG THE SPECTRUM

MISSED OPPORTUNITIES AND LOST DISCOVERIES

Many years ago, during a family trip to Colorado, a friend told me a story that provides an inside look at how scientists work. I was just beginning serious research for my first book and we were discussing creativity and the process of discovery. He was a well-known cancer researcher and taught at the University of Colorado in Boulder. He told me he would sometimes prefer to forget this story. I asked if it had ever been written down anywhere. He said no. He and all of his associates found it too upsetting to recall or record—but he told me it was alright for me to tell the story.

Years ago, one of his friends was a young researcher in a biochemistry laboratory and was performing a procedure intended to destroy DNA, the molecular blueprint for self-replication carried in all living cells. She was annoyed, however, at not being able to make the procedure work as intended. Each time she measured the results of her work, she came up with more DNA than she started with. The researcher tried again and again. But each time she was disappointed to discover that she had more DNA rather than less once again. Her coworkers were sympathetic and tried to help her. But no solution to the problem could be found. She eventually dropped the project and went on to other tasks.

Some years later, another scientist in a different laboratory successfully developed a new method to create DNA, making many copies—and he subsequently received a Nobel Prize for his discovery. The young researcher and her former colleagues are still asking themselves how it is that they did not recognize what was really going on when her project repeatedly failed.[1]

The story of the second scientist is now well known in scientific circles. The discoverer was Kary B. Mullis, who shared the 1993 Nobel Prize in Chemistry with another scientist, Michael Smith. Mullis received the prize for his development of the Polymerase Chain Reaction (PCR) that makes it possible to rapidly make thousands or millions of copies of specific DNA sequences. The improvements provided by Mullis have made the PCR technique of central importance in molecular biology and biochemistry. According to the Nobel Prize presentation at the Royal Swedish Academy of Sciences: "Using this method it is possible to amplify and isolate in a test tube a specific DNA segment within a background of a complex gene pool. In this repetitive process the number of copies of the specific DNA segment doubles during each cycle. In a few hours it is possible to achieve more than 20 cycles, which produces over a million copies."[2]

Of course, the story is so upsetting because she had the discovery right there in front of her, but she was so focused on her seemingly failed project that she could not see the value of her experiment's results. Such stories teach us. Sometimes a gift is seen only as a problem, something that would be quickly wished away had we the power. Sometimes the most important thing is to be able to recognize the gift for what it is, even though it was not requested or desired. For this to be possible, it is helpful (in spite of one's training) not to be wholly focused on the narrow interests of the moment—no matter how serious the task, no matter how large the grant, no matter how urgent the deadline. One has to be open to new possibilities, to looking at things a different way, to being able to see what you have been given, even when it is not what you asked for.

The role of chance or fortuitous accident is one of several themes that recur repeatedly in the literature of creativity, especially creativity in the sciences. I do not assume that all creativity is necessarily associated with some form of learning disability or learning difference. However, I do believe that a number of traits associated with dyslexia, other learning differences, and especially high visual-spatial talents may tend to predispose some individuals to greater creativity than might exist otherwise.

Being able to do what others want you to do, in the way they want you to do it, is seductive. If you can, you will. But if you cannot, you will have to find another way. It is a form of accidental self-selection. If it is possible to do it in the same way, successfully, often a new way will not be tried. Thus, if a truly original method is needed, the conventionally successful student or researcher may be the last one to find it. Sometimes only among those who have repeatedly failed is there a high likelihood of success.

A PECULIAR AFFLICTION

There are many stories of unusual problems or situations that lead to important discoveries in science, engineering and technology. one of the most interesting examples is that of Nikola Tesla, the engineer, who, among many other things, created the alternating current electric power system that we use all around the world today. As a young man, Tesla had an "peculiar affliction." He explains: "In my boyhood I suffered from a peculiar affliction due to the appearance of images, often accompanied by strong flashes of light, which marred the sight of real objects and interfered with my thought and action."[3] He makes clear that although these images were powerful in their projection, they were not hallucinations. "They were pictures of things and scenes which I had really seen, never of those I had imagined. When a word was spoken to me the image of the object it designated would present itself vividly to my vision and sometimes I was quite unable to distinguish whether what I saw was tangible or not. This caused me great discomfort and anxiety. . . . These certainly were not hallucinations . . . for in other respects I was normal and composed."

THINKING IN PICTURES

Nikola Telsa has long been of special interest for me because of his extraordinarily powerful visual imagination. As he says, his imagination appears to have been so highly developed that he could create complete models of devices in his mind, building them and running them as if they were real machines. But it is probably of no small consequence that he seems to have experienced, initially, this powerful ability to visualize things not as a useful talent or wonderful gift but, as we have seen, as a problem instead.

The son of a Serbian Orthodox priest, Tesla was relatively well educated in literature, science, and mathematics and had a strong practical inventive inclination. He was a lonely man with many odd habits and strong compulsions. For example, at each meal he would have to calculate the cubic area of each bite of food before eating it. Similarly, he had to finish reading whatever he started, even when it ran into many volumes, whether or not he had lost interest or had decided that he was getting little in return for his effort.

In 1884, he immigrated to America during a time of great excitement over technical innovation with the telephone, electric lights, and other new inventions. He even worked for Thomas Edison for a while (with extraordinary energy and dedication) when he first arrived in America. But he finally left Edison's company to pursue his own highly innovative but incompatible ideas—inventing, eventually, the entire alternating current electric power system used around the world today. He sold the rights to this system to Westinghouse for a few thousand dollars. Sadly, if he had retained shares, he would never have had the money and patronage problems that he endured for most of his life.

In order to control his strong visual imagination in his youth, Tesla experimented with various mental exercises and, quite literally, flights of the imagination. In time, it became clear that the "affliction" was the negative side of what turned out to be a special and unusual talent. He continued these exercises

until I was about seventeen when my thoughts turned seriously to invention. Then I observed to my delight that I could visualize with the greatest facility. I needed no models, drawings or experiments. I could picture them all as real in my mind. Thus I have been led unconsciously to evolve what I consider a new method of materializing inventive concepts and ideas, which is radically opposite to the purely experimental and is in my opinion ever so much more expeditious and efficient.

When I get an idea I start at once building it up in my imagination. I change the construction, make improvements and operate the device in my mind. It is absolutely immaterial to me whether I run my turbine in thought or test it in my shop. I even note if it is out of balance. There is no difference whatever; the results were the same. In this way I am able to rapidly develop and perfect a conception without touching anything. When I have gone so far to embody in the invention every possible improvement I can think of and see no fault anywhere, I put into concrete form this final product of my brain. Invariably my device works as I conceived that it should, and the experiment comes out exactly as I planned it. In twenty years there has not been a single exception.[4]

Tesla explains that if something is constructed before it is fully developed and worked out in the mind, then the experimenter is often distracted by comparatively unimportant details of apparatus construction. In Tesla's words: "The moment one constructs a device to carry into practice a crude idea he finds himself unavoidably engrossed with the details and defects of the apparatus. As he goes on improving and reconstructing, his force of concentration diminishes and he loses sight of the great underlying principle...."

POWERS BEYOND BELIEF

Some might question Tesla's claims. He was known to have a tendency to make extravagant statements, especially to eager young reporters. We know also that Tesla was a great showman when demonstrating his new electrical devices to the public—more like a magician than an engineer or scientist. Yet his tricks were based on scientific and engineering knowledge that was not known by others in his field until decades later. Also, many of the extravagant tales and devices, like laser beams, long-distance microwave power transmission, and ocean thermal electricity generation, are only comparatively recently coming into serious consideration and use.

For many, Tesla's claims were hard to believe (although those who did believe in him, in contrast, accorded him almost cult leader–like status). However, we now have reason for taking Tesla at his word. He does provide some justification for why this should be so: "Why should it be otherwise? Engineering, electrical and mechanical, is positive in results. There is scarcely a subject that cannot be mathematically treated and the effects calculated or the results determined beforehand from the available theoretical and practical data. The carrying out into practice of a crude idea as is being generally done is, I hold, nothing but a waste of energy, money and time."[5]

MODELS IN MIND AND MACHINE

We are now learning that Tesla can be believed, in most respects. It is perhaps a sign of our times that what might be seen as a bizarre tale spun by Tesla in a magazine article published in 1919, is now, nearly one hundred years later, exploding into prominence at the center of industry and commerce. Tesla argued that it is a waste of time and money to build a model or prototype of anything until a number of variations have been tested in a powerful visual imagination such as his own. Virtually the same point is being made in most recent years by designers, engineers, and managers—but this time they are talking about the machine equivalent of Tesla's remarkable and unusual imagination—that is, what is now known as "3-D computing" and the associated "3-D printing."

With three-dimensional computing, working models of aircraft, automobiles, golf clubs, or nuclear power plants can be constructed inside a powerful graphic computer and displayed on a screen—with parts manufactured or "printed" as needed. These models can be operated and tested and modified much as Tesla was apparently able to do with his imagination alone. The inventor may have the concept clearly in mind, but he or she needs the visual tools to convey the concept to others.

Proponents claim many advantages for the widespread use of 3-D computing, but two of the most important advantages relate to increased creativity and reductions in the costs of prototype building. For example, in one early study of the use of 3-D computing in several US and Japanese companies: "The speed and power of 3-D Computing has all but eliminated the requirements to produce physical prototypes and models. This allows management and engineers to economically pursue more creative and sometimes high-risk design options. NASA Ames uses [3-D] workstations to simulate a wide number of options for a Mach 25 aircraft that would have been cost prohibitive using the traditional wind tunnel practices."[6]

Tesla noted the speed and ease with which his mental modeling proceeded, free of the distractions of building an actual physical prototype. This is not an unusual observation. Creative designers often lament the time required to build a physical product of what could be built so quickly in their minds. Thus, it may not be surprising that, in practice, another important consequence of 3-D computing continues to be a marked decrease in frustration along with a marked increase in productivity:

> Users of 3D Computing reported increases in individual's productivity of 20 percent to 50 percent. This higher productivity was used to expand the scope of individual job functions and to reduce the actual time to complete a project. The ability to "handle" the realistic electronic model led to improved interaction between the designer and the model, resulting in a more intimate and accurate understanding of the model. This also resulted in more creativity. We consistently observed that users had a positive work attitude and they preferred working in a 3D environment as compared to the manual or 2D environment in which they had previously worked.[7]

This kind of report makes one wonder whether 3-D computing is just one more step in an old progression or whether these developments, by now well established, should be seen as the beginning of something that is really quite new. Such changes may make it possible for comparatively ordinary people to do with ease and speed what before only extraordinary people like Tesla could do inside their heads. And, as we have noted before, this new direction in development might very well favor those who are much better with the manipulation of images than the manipulation of words, numbers, and even mathematical symbols.

With Tesla, the power of the visual imagination takes on a whole new dimension. He was clearly an intensely creative visual thinker. He had some related difficulties, such as a curious inability to make drawings, but these did not appear to be a problem for him. Perhaps his greatest liability was his fierce independence and lack of social skills that repeatedly caused him to fall out with his coworkers and benefactors, eventually making him unable to continue his work.

Telsa, however, provides us with an example of visual thinking that illustrates, in a most concrete way, the power and potential of this ability. What Faraday, Maxwell, and Einstein may have been able to do with abstract images, imaginary mechanical analogies, or related mathematical formulas, Tesla seems to have been able to do in his mind with almost real mechanical devices and working machinery. Tesla provides us not only with important new insights but also with a standard against which other visual thinkers may be assessed. He also provides us with an example of what, in time, more ordinary people may be able to do with the new tools that are becoming cheaper, more powerful, and easier to use as they become more and more widely available.

THINKING IN PICTURES IN ANOTHER DIMENSION

I decided to include Nikola in my earlier book *In the Mind's Eye* because of his wonderful descriptions of his own powerful visualization abilities—in spite of the fact that he had no indication of the language-related learning problems I was also interested in. He had many unusual characteristics, but he seemed in most respects entirely unlike most of the other individuals I had researched in writing that book. I suspected that there was a significant pattern to Tesla's unusual mixture of traits, but I had no idea what it was. Then I read Temple Grandin's book *Thinking in Pictures*. Grandin, who is autistic herself, describes the traits typically seen in a form of high-functioning autism (until recently) known as "Asperger's syndrome." In one chapter she deals with the possible relationship of giftedness or even genius in relation to the syndrome. Here she describes a number of important historical figures who would appear to have many of the appropriate traits. Although she does not explicitly name Tesla, it would appear that Grandin had clearly supplied the pattern I had been looking for. Common characteristics of Asperger's syndrome have been given as: excellent rote memory, notable lack of social skills and lack of sensitivity to various social cues, strong focus, and single-mindedness of thought and action along with eccentric, sometimes compulsive behavior. All of these would appear to fit what we know of Nikola Tesla.

As many are aware, in recent years, there has been an explosion of interest in autism and Asperger's syndrome. This increase in interest is mainly due to apparent very large increases in the numbers of children (and their parents) being diagnosed. The causes and use of this diagnosis continue to be hotly debated. However, certain patterns seem clear enough. By now it is well known that these increases in numbers are often associated with areas of the country where many high technology industries are located.

A now classic article by Steve Silberman for *Wired* magazine, titled "The Geek Syndrome," summarized the situation:

> At clinics and schools in [Silicon] Valley, the observation that most parents of autistic kids are engineers and programmers who themselves display autistic behavior is not news. And it may not be news to other communities either. Last January, Microsoft became the first major U.S. corporation to offer its employees insurance benefits to cover the cost of behavioral training for their autistic children. One Bay Area mother [reported] that when she was planning a move to Minnesota with her son, who has Asperger's syndrome, she asked the school district there if they could meet her son's needs. "They told me that the northwest quadrant of Rochester, where the IBMers congregate, has a large number of Asperger kids," she recalls. "It was recommended I move to that part of town."[8]

Links with a range of technical occupations have been widely observed. Some call Asperger's syndrome "the engineers' disorder." Certain high-tech entrepreneurs and company heads are sometimes linked to the condition as well. Silberman's article in *Wired* notes that "Bill Gates is regularly diagnosed in the press: His single-minded focus on technical minutiae, rocking motions, and flat tone of voice are all suggestive of an adult with some trace of the disorder." Strong visual traits are not necessarily a major component of autism or Asperger's syndrome. However, for both Nikola Tesla and Temple Grandin herself (and others), visualization and visual thinking are central components of their thought processes.

In April 2004, an article in the *New York Times* by Amy Harmon focused on the rapidly spreading awareness of Asperger's syndrome among adults with the condition. Most had long been puzzled by the traits in themselves but did not know, until much later, that there was a diagnosis and a name for their way of processing and interacting with the world. They thought they were alone.

Now many are gathering together in support groups. Harmon observes:

> They all share a defining trait: They are what autism researchers call "mind blind." Lacking the ability to read cues like body language to intuit what other people are thinking, they have profound difficulty navigating basic social interactions. The diagnosis is reordering their lives. Some have become newly determined to learn how to compensate. They are filling up scarce classes that teach skills like how close to stand next to someone at a party, or how to tell when people are angry even when they are smiling. The then new and rapidly spreading awareness had many effects in many directions, especially within families. . . . This new wave of discovery . . . is also sending ripples through the lives of their families, soothing tension among some married couples, prompting others to call it quits. Parents who saw their adult

children as lost causes or black sheep are fumbling for ways to help them, suddenly realizing that they are disabled, not stubborn or lazy.[9]

Also, Harmon observed that the support groups were having important effects on those affected: "Some are finding solace in support groups where they are meeting others like themselves for the first time. And a growing number are beginning to celebrate their own unique way of seeing the world. They question the superiority of people they call 'neurotypicals' . . . and challenge them to adopt a more enlightened, gentle outlook toward social eccentricities."

It is a remarkable fact that a much acclaimed and bestselling mystery novel, *The Curious Incident of the Dog in the Night-Time* by Mark Haddon, very much in evidence in the spring of 2004 in bookshops in both the United States and Britain, had as narrator a fifteen-year-old boy with Asperger's syndrome. Haddon, who had some early work experience with autism and similar conditions, explains that he really chanced upon the flat "voice" of the narrator—who loves mathematics and patterns and describes exactly what he is seeing but never fully understands its social significance. Haddon said that when he chanced upon this voice and realized how useful it would be to himself as writer, he thought he had something very special: "When you're writing in that voice, you never try and persuade the reader to feel this or that about something. And once I realized that, I knew that the voice was gold dust."

WITH TESLA, FROM VISUALIZATION TO ASPERGER'S SYNDROME, NEVER PLANNED

We started out with the story of Nikola Tesla helping us to understand the great power of certain forms of visual imagination and visualization. Then, his story served as a bridge to help us understand the possibilities as new computer visualization systems extend some of this visualization power to individuals who have conventional brains but access to unconventionally powerful machines. But beyond this, never in the original plan, we are then led to see that many aspects of Tesla's strange behavior and his remarkable talents can be better understood in the context of the relatively recently recognized patterns in autism and Asperger's syndrome.

The term *autism* was first described and named in the 1940s (by two separate individuals) while the term *Asperger's syndrome* did not appear in US diagnostic manuals until the 1990s. (Even more recently, the term *Asperger's syndrome* has been dropped by certain professional groups, but it is still in active use by many in the field.) Both forms were once thought to be extremely rare, until, just in the last few years, large increases in incidence became evident and demanded attention.

Tesla's example has helped us understand a new way of seeing the world—one that would appear to be closely linked to the use of the newest visual technologies. Yet, remarkably, it would appear that there is a new recognition of whole groups of children and adults who would seem to be more or less like Tesla, especially in those parts of the country where the newest technologies are being created and developed.

Some argue that the usual process (and numbers) of children with "autism spectrum" disorders is increased because these new technology centers tend to draw together (and reward highly) large numbers of those having few or moderate autistic traits. As a consequence, it is said, some of the affected adults then marry each other (in larger numbers than would have happened otherwise), and then they have children who may have autistic traits that are much more pronounced than either parent alone (a process known as "assortative mating.")

Dr. Dan Geschwind, director of the neurogenetics lab at UCLA, has seen some similarities between dyslexia and autism, since both challenge conventional ideas about human intelligence:

Certain kinds of excellence might require not just various modes of thinking, but different kinds of brains. "Autism gets to fundamental issues of how we view talents and disabilities," he says. "The flip side of dyslexia is [may be having, with reading problems] enhanced abilities in math and architecture. There may be an aspect of this going on with autism and assortative mating in places like Silicon Valley. In the parents, who carry a few of the genes, they're a good thing. In the kids, who carry too many, it's very bad."[10]

COMING TO A NEW UNDERSTANDING

As a new awareness comes into public consciousness through various sources like Grandin's books (and HBO film), Silberman's *Wired* article, or Haddon's novel, it is hoped that all of us will develop a better understanding about why some people behave the way that they do—as well as gain some insight into how they are able to do things the rest of us cannot do. We may become more tolerant, or we may come to be more aware of the power of real diversity. Or, we may be more willing to have certain services available for affected children and adults. Some may be more inclined to see some of these traits in ourselves or our friends or our family members.

Whatever our reaction, it gradually becomes apparent that we may be on the edge of not one but two major changes. The new visual and other technologies may allow us to use our brains in far more powerful ways than the conventional technologies of words and numbers and books alone. But at the same time, without being fully aware of what we are doing and how we are doing it, we may be helping to create larger numbers of individuals who are unusually well suited to work within these new worlds. It may be far too early to understand what is going on here or what it signifies. However, there do seem to be parallels with past dyslexia research that could be helpful.

PARADOX AND SOCIAL BENEFIT

Dyslexia was first recognized and described more than a century ago, in the 1880s, some sixty years before autism was described. Like autism, it was initially thought to be extremely rare. Now it is seen as affecting up to 15 to 20 percent of the population, depending on the definitions used—and as having profound effects on education, employment, and life success. There was little scientific or government attention to dyslexia until the last few decades when both increased greatly, with substantial funding for research. Throughout, there has always been a tendency to look at the *problems* associated with dyslexia, and the focus has been on ways to fix the problems. But also, from the earliest days, there has been a very small group of individuals who believed that with the dyslexia came certain advantages (sometimes, or even often—but not always).

Among these was the late Harvard neurologist Dr. Norman Geschwind (a distant relative of Dan Geschwind, quoted above). He believed that the same unusual neurological formations that lead to dyslexia could also promote a range of superior abilities. Accordingly, he has provided a discussion that also may have some relevance to autism spectrum disorders: If the problem condition also has advantages (in some cases), he wondered, then how can we learn to control the condition and not give up the (sometimes considerable) advantages? Norman Geschwind's comments on the possible prevention of dyslexia take on an extra dimension of significance when we consider autism as well. Geschwind explains: "the dilemma...becomes obvious. Not only do many dyslexics carry remarkable talents that benefit their society enormously, but the same talents exist in unusually high frequency among their unaffected relatives. If we could somehow prevent these brain changes, and thus prevent the appearance of dyslexia, might we not find that we have deprived the society of an important and irreplaceable group of individuals endowed with remarkable talents?"[11]

In spite of this, Geschwind was hopeful that the advantages and disadvantages are not necessarily connected. This hope was based on evidence that there are many non-dyslexic "individuals among the relatives of dyslexics who are ... possessed of remarkable spatial talents. ... We know that especially frequently the sisters of dyslexics are likely to share the talents without the disadvantages of dyslexia. Once we gain intimate information as to the mechanisms of formation of the anomalies that lead to the superior talents, we should be able to retain the advantages while avoiding the disadvantages."

Thus, Geschwind hoped to have, eventually, one without the other. We too may well hope for this (with dyslexia and with autism), but we need also to consider the possibility that it may not always be possible to siphon off only the advantages. We may need to consider that it may be an essential part of the nature of things that, in a significant number of cases, we cannot have one without the other.

Is it possible that our brains have such design constraints? Is it possible that unusual proficiency in one area will often mean a significant lack of proficiency in another? Or, conversely, is it possible that a deficiency in one area may indicate the likelihood of special abilities in other areas? Or, given a third case, if one has fairly balanced capabilities, is it probable that, in many instances, extraordinary abilities (in either of two incompatible modes) may be precluded? Most recent neurological evidence suggests that this may in fact be so.

Albert Galaburda, an associate of Norman Geschwind, years ago, carried out microanatomical studies of the brains of dyslexics. After detailed examination of several cases, Galaburda and his associates described the role of microscopic lesions (areas of damage or diminished growth) and the unusual symmetry of certain formations that had been observed in all of the dyslexic brains that they had examined. Galaburda observed that the microscopic lesions may be capable of suppressing the development of some areas, but he suggested a role for them in actually increasing the development of other areas. This research suggests a biological basis for the frequent paradoxical coexistence of special abilities and disabilities in the same individual: "We all know that these lesions may in fact be capable of reorganizing the brain. But they don't always reorganize the brain to produce dyslexics. I am sure that similar mechanisms are used to reorganize the brain to produce geniuses too, and sometimes both of them occur in the same person."[12]

Norman Geschwind pointed out that the study of dyslexia is filled with paradoxes. If the observations of Geschwind and Galaburda are borne out by further research, then perhaps one of the most striking paradoxes is that many of those with the greatest abilities can also be expected to have unusual difficulty in areas that are easy for those with average abilities. Similarly, we could find that the study of Asperger's syndrome and other autism spectrum disorders may also be filled with paradoxes—the greatest of which may be, when we come to learn more about autism (as with dyslexia), is it possible that we may find that we cannot live entirely without it, at least in some moderate measure? As Dan Geschwind noted above, these studies tend to take us to deeper levels, forcing us (as did Tesla's story) to think in fresh ways about human intelligence and capability.

SIMILAR OBSERVATIONS ABOUT VISUAL THINKING— TEMPLE GRANDIN

Although my research and writing has always focused mainly on dyslexia, visual thinking, and visual technologies, gradually my attention has shifted to Asperger's syndrome and autism. I first read of Temple Grandin in Oliver Sacks's book *An Anthropologist on Mars*. And, over the years, I have been impressed with the work she has done to educate the public about Asperger's syndrome and autism—with her books and many talks, especially in places like Google and the TED venues, many of which are readily available on YouTube. It is a delight to hear her address her remarks to the "geeks" in the audience and hear the knowing laughter. And, of course, her now well-known life story on HBO has educated many thousands. Not so well known are her books on social skills and career options for those with Asperger's syndrome or autism. These are treasures and a great public service—as are her books and her designs and measurement scales for the humane treatment of animals.[13]

Some years ago, I found Grandin's wonderful book *Thinking in Pictures*. Although, as noted previously, dyslexia and Asperger's syndrome appear to be quite different, it seemed to me that the strong visual aspect observed in members of each group had to mean something. I wondered what it might be. When Temple was on her book tour promoting the paperback edition of *Thinking in Pictures*, she came to Washington, DC, for a book signing and a lecture to an autism parent group.

At the book signing, I stood in line after her talk and asked her to sign the copy of her book that I had just purchased (although I had already bought and read a different copy). At the same time, I took the liberty of presenting her with a copy of my own book, *In the Mind's Eye*, which I thought she might find interesting. She took one look at my book and said that she had always wanted to read it. I asked how she knew of it. She said that she had seen a review of my book when she was correcting the proofs for *Thinking in Pictures* and found it quite interesting. It was too late to put anything more into her own text, but she could add a book to her list of suggested readings—where, to my surprise, she pointed it out—following the first chapter. (Later she listed my book on her own list of all-time favorites—and, later still, she provided me with a blurb for the second edition of *In the Mind's Eye*.) The next afternoon, we had a long telephone conversation about the similarities and differences between her treatment of visual thinking in relation to autism and my treatment of visual thinking in relation to dyslexia.

I had always hoped to look more into these connections, but whenever I brought it up to researchers in the field, I was told that the two conditions were too dissimilar. Nothing could be learned, they explained, from looking at them together. For some time, I have suspected that they could be wrong. I thought that the high visual aspect in two rather different but overlapping conditions might lead to some insight both unexpected and valuable. (Perhaps more valuable because unexpected.) I am still wondering whether we may come to see, one way or the other, in the not-too-distant future whether my hunch might be correct.

I have become a great admirer of Temple's books, especially *The Autistic Brain: Thinking Across the Spectrum.* I was particularly interested to see her treatment of the way talents and abilities among autistic individuals are frequently misunderstood—not unlike a similar problem among professionals in the dyslexia field. According to Temple:

> A few years ago, Michelle Dawson, an autism researcher . . . at the University of Montréal, asked herself an important question. Her research on the autistic brain, like the other autism research at the clinic, like autism research everywhere, focused on cognitive impairment—on what was wrong. And she realized that when an autistic person exhibited characteristics that we would call strengths if they belong to a normal person, we still saw those strengths as merely the fortunate byproduct of bad wiring. *But what if they're not?* she asked herself. What if they're not the byproducts of bad wiring? What if they're not the *byproducts* of anything? What if, instead, they're simply the *products* of wiring—wiring that's neither good nor bad? . . . And even when a study does recognize strength in autistic subjects, the authors often regarded it as the brain's way of compensating for a deficit.[14]

Fortunately, Grandin is able to report "a new attitude toward autism." She noted that special abilities had always been reported but rarely researched. More recently, as one researcher observed, "Now they're beginning to develop interest in those [reported] strengths to help us understand autism."[15]

EXPLODING GUITARS AND ADVENTURES WITH CUBBY—JOHN ELDER ROBISON

In the early years, Robison had mostly been a "roadie" for rock bands. When he was a teenager, he had dropped out of high school and worked obsessively (in typical Asperger's syndrome fashion) with electronic circuits—including the sounds that different circuits could make and their waveforms on an oscilloscope. He became very good at this. Subsequently, for a time Robison repaired the amplifiers for a rock group that rented out their equipment when they were not on tour (Pink Floyd). In time, he was asked to help groups when on tour—helping them to make sounds never heard before—and making guitars that would explode and burn on stage, but not injure the performer or the audience: "I got hired by KISS, where we made Ace Frehley's signature fire-breathing, rocket-firing, and disco-lighted guitars. It was a good life, but unpredictable."[16] Later, Robison designed sounds for toys and games at Milton Bradley and, later still, started his own auto service, repair, and restoration business, specializing in imported up-market cars. Throughout, he was working as a high-level expert, but he was always uncomfortable because he was working among engineers and technicians but had no qualifications—and he strongly disliked the conventional corporate persona. This is the reason, he says, that he started his own auto service business.

I first met Robison at a conference called Diamonds in the Rough.

We were both scheduled to speak. At a brief, informal book signing, John stopped by to purchase a copy of *In the Mind's Eye*. I decided to attend his talk that afternoon, during which he mostly talked about his first book, *Look Me in the Eye*. Later I attended several of his talks in the DC area—talks given to NIH researchers, to parents, to teachers, and to young students with Asperger's syndrome. I always thought I gained useful insights in listening to the talks and the questions. One night, in response to a question, John talked about his experience with TMS (transcranial magnetic stimulation) and how it brought back vividly his early work with circuits and music, and, more important, opened a door for his perception of emotions. Some time later, Robison's book came out which told the story: *Switched On—A Memoir of Brain Change and Emotional Awakening*.[17]

As a person with Asperger's syndrome, John Elder Robison is also, similar to Temple Grandin, interested in the often-misunderstood advantages and talents. His son, whom he calls "Cubby," also has Asperger's syndrome. Robison observes that there are many books about children with Asperger's written by parents who document their long struggle to gain appropriate educational and medical services. In contrast, Robison said was mainly interested in the fun he has had with his son. His book, *Raising Cubby*, has the long subtitle: *A Father and Son's Adventures with Asperger's, Trains, Tractors, and High Explosives*.

Of course, Robison notes many problems, but he focuses mainly on the fun. Both father and his young son were interested in mechanical things, preferably big mechanical things—train-switching yards, harbor ship-loading cranes, and the like. They had relatively easy access for switching yards and other places near their home in western Massachusetts. They were so well known in one switching yard that one engineer invited the little boy to drive the locomotive for a bit.

However, other locations were more difficult, and they were turned away. Then Robison, a great storyteller, hit upon an idea. They would not be so easily turned away if the guards and local yard managers believed that the little boy was an important owner of the company. So they bought ten shares of the railroad company stock and showed up at the gate, asking for a tour, with the company annual report in hand. They were traveling in a thirty-year-old Rolls-Royce Silver Shadow that Robison had bought cheaply at auction and had fixed up in his high-end auto repair and restoration business. As Robison noted, "You get a lot more respect in a Rolls-Royce than you do in a regular car, no matter who you are."[18] The guard was impressed. "Instead of challenging our presence in the yard, he became what you might call cautiously deferential." The guard called in the "general manager of yard, who knelt down very seriously and ceremoniously and shook Cubby's hand. . . . He asked how many shares he owned, and Cubby smiled enigmatically." They got their tour and had many other adventures—especially later when Cubby, a bit older, became interested in chemistry. . . .

Different thinkers may have many problems. But Temple Grandin and John Elder Robison show us what is possible when you see things differently and do things differently—by seeing what others do not see or cannot see.

Chapter Four

THE POWER OF DESIGN

"... He's uncomfortable knowing that hundred thousand Apple employees rely on his decision-making—his taste—and that a sudden announcement of his retirement would ambush Apple shareholders. (To take a number: a ten-percent drop in Apple's valuation represents seventy-one billion dollars.) According to Laurene Powell Jobs, Steve Jobs's widow, who is close to Ive and his family, "Jony's an artist with an artist's temperament, and he'd be the first to tell you artists aren't supposed to be responsible for this kind of thing."[1]

Jony Ive, head of design at Apple has long felt the pressure of success. Year after year, commentators have predicted that Apple's winning product line would not continue. After the iMac, the iPod, the iPhone, and the iPad, they would knowingly predict that the line would end. But since Steve Jobs's return to the company in 1997, the series of successful products has largely continued, even after Jobs's death in 2011. Recognized as the most valuable company in the world, Apple has built its reputation on continuous innovation and high quality. In many ways, this success is based on the work of British-trained designer Jony Ive.

In spite of frequent adverse predictions, and occasional difficulties, Apple seems to be maintaining its coveted position. In early February 2017, a newspaper story announced: "In case you had started to doubt it: people still love the iPhone. Apple announced Tuesday that it had sold 78.2 million iPhones in its first fiscal quarter—a record for any quarter in the company's history."[2]

The continued success of Ive's work at Apple has also brought the work of the designer to center stage. Too often in the past, the designer's work had relatively low impact and relatively low prestige. The designer's job was to put a box around a product that had been specified by engineers under the guidance of marketing and financial leadership. Working with Steve Jobs, Jony Ive carved out an entirely new role. The new position of the designer would be at the center. The new role of the designer would be the integration of everything—appearance, functionality, hardware, engineering, manufacturing, software, tone of advertising, everything. The new role vastly increased the power and prestige of the industrial designer. Steve Jobs told his biographer: "[Ive] has more operational power than anyone else at Apple except me."[3]

Clearly, Jony Ive is a strong visual thinker. He shared with Jobs a minimalist approach to design, emphasizing simplicity and functionality. Ive says that as he travels he is always looking at manufactured objects, how they are made, how they function—and whether they are designed and crafted with care. These are traits that are familiar among visual-thinking dyslexics and different thinkers. Ive's unofficial biographer says that Ive is dyslexic; but we don't have a lot of detail.[4] Whether or not this is correct, it seems clear enough that the pattern would not be unexpected. For example, the British architect Richard Rogers and the late American architect Hugh Newell Jacobson are both dyslexic and have talked about it freely for years. Among designers and architects, dyslexia is not surprising. Dyslexic designers, architects, and other forms of artists may exhibit certain approaches to their work that may not be difficult to identify.

THE "WOW" FACTOR—SEEING THE DIFFERENCE IN SEEING

Once one begins to understand varied patterns of dyslexic difficulties and talents, one can often see the possibility of dyslexia with very brief observations. The Harvard neurologist Norman Geschwind noted that one could see the possibility through the talents observed at a very early age—seeing the preschool child who was much better at blocks than the other children.

The dyslexic molecular biologist William Dreyer told me, as we have noted, that he enjoyed trying to discover the hidden dyslexics among his fellow professors at the California Institute of Technology. He said there were few, but you could usually tell just by the way they talked and explained their ideas. He also suggested that they were likely to be more creative in their professional accomplishments.

A similar approach has been taken by Drs. Brock and Fernette Eide, the authors of the book *The Dyslexic Advantage*. In the blog at DyslexicAdvantage.org, Fernette observed that it was the special and distinctive forms of talent that showed them that dyslexia was not only a pathology. In a recent brief website blog post, Fernette wrote about one of the first things that made them question whether dyslexia was really "just a disorder":

> It was when we realized we could often spot a dyslexic person based on something they did really well, not just from their problems. We'd see an invention, or a building, or a movie, or a business, and it would have a certain kind of "flair" or "flavor"—a "wow" factor—that suggested it could only come from a mind that worked in really different and wonderful ways. A mind that made connections most of us couldn't see. We found that the more unique and innovative it was—the bigger the leap from what had come before—the greater the odds it came from a dyslexic mind.[5]

They noted that "this 'wow' factor works [in] the world of architecture. You can see it in other fields, as well. Think about product design. The Apple products of the last two decades that are the work of lead designer Jony Ive. James Dyson's innovative vacuums or hand dryers or air purifiers. Dean Kamen's Segway or stair-climbing wheelchair. These products share the 'extreme creativity' that seems to come so often from dyslexic minds."[6]

Fernette finishes the post with one of their favorite examples of "reverse diagnosis"—through strengths rather than difficulties.

> When we were writing our book, *The Dyslexic Advantage*, we were looking for a perfect example of [a dyslexic designer]. . . . One person who came immediately to mind was David Kelley, a legend in the world of design. Kelley built the first Apple mouse for Steve Jobs, and founded both IDEO, one of the world's leading design firms, and the Stanford design school (Institute of Design). We were huge fans of Kelley's work on creativity and design, and felt certain from the way his mind worked that he must be dyslexic. [The] only problem was, we couldn't find any mention of dyslexia in all our research about him. So we chose to write about other folks. . . . Shortly after our book was published we attended a talk Kelley gave. Afterwards someone asked if he'd ever written down the things he was sharing. "Oh no," he said with a chuckle, "I'm horribly dyslexic—I never write if I can help it!"[7]

Accordingly, Brock and Fernette Eide, who through their clinical practice know a great deal about testing and diagnosis, often find it easy to see the possibility of dyslexia in cases of extreme creative talent, especially in invention, art, architecture, design, and related occupations.

I, myself, have had many similar experiences, including the famous mathematician Benoit Mandelbrot (I suspected that he might be dyslexic; and he confirmed my suspicion, in a roundabout way), and even my mother's first cousin, the famous movie stunt pilot, the late Frank

Gifford Tallman (his dyslexia was confirmed by information supplied by his younger sister).

ALWAYS DESIGNING—CAROLYN HUBBARD-FORD

I have been focusing on the apparent frequency of dyslexia among various kinds of designers and other strong visual thinkers. But, of course, one does not have to be dyslexic to be a successful designer. A friend who is a successful designer herself, Carolyn Hubbard-Ford, helped me to understand this. A few years ago my wife, Margaret, and I were visiting Carolyn and her husband, Jonathan, in London. We started chatting about the design of various projects, and Carolyn offered to jot down some ideas that might or might not be useful to explain to me how a designer works and how they see the world. We arranged to go through her list of notes, with my iPhone recording.[8] We came up with a number of obvious observations—and some not-so-obvious.

Originally from Guernsey in the British Channel Islands, Carolyn first came to London as a young fashion designer. She designed a line of knitted dresses that were so successful that the entire manufacturing order was sold out of the main London store. None were available for the regional stores, so they had to go back to the manufacturers several times. Carolyn eventually moved to Hong Kong and focused on interior design and eventually real estate. Returning to London, she focused on restoring properties and all aspects of design, including space planning, built-in items, and custom-made furniture. She also took up painting, self-taught, sometimes deliberately imitating the art of well-known artists. She took delight when family members of the artists and professional experts thought the canvases in her home were originals—before she explained that it was her own work—and unsigned.

She also painted a number of canvases of her own design. Some of these were available on web-based image services. I was especially impressed that one of her paintings was selected for the cover of the Vintage Random House reissue of Aldous Huxley's 1932 classic, *Brave New World*. On the back of the book it says, "Cover: detail from *City in Shards of Light* by Carolyn Hubbard-Ford. Private collection/Bridgemen Art Library." I recall how pleased I was when I happened to visit a major bookstore near Oxford University and saw a wall full of Carolyn's artwork on the shelves. The reissue had just been released.

Carolyn made several observations about the way she worked. It was not surprising that she told me that her highly visual mind, not unlike Jony Ive's, seems always to be looking around and redesigning the objects and buildings she sees, trying to work out better solutions. When at the theater or at restaurants, she finds herself redesigning the whole environment—the theater sets or ways to make the restaurant more attractive: "It does not feel good and it didn't have to be like that, " she says. Much of her design work, for a property, a painting, or a piece of furniture, will be done in her head, at, say, 3:00–5:00 am, while lying in bed, mulling it over in detail. The whole design will be gone through, fully visualized, corrections made. The design will be ready to record the next morning. Sometimes notes are jotted down in the middle of the night, if the details are complicated and might be forgotten. Carolyn thought everyone did this and was surprised to learn that they didn't.

She also explained that when she has to select a code for a safe, or a lift, she will often choose a pattern or shape that the buttons suggest, not a number, as it's easier to recall. Similarly, a close look at the map for a destination is more useful to her, as this is what will be recalled more easily than the actual address in words and numbers. She finds that she is very aware of body language, especially when she hears a politician saying one thing but the body language says something else. She says it is something like negative space in art composition—not looking at the object but looking at the space around the object. "I put big store by my ability to read body language. The eyes give much away."

She maintains a sizeable library of images that she relates to in some particular way—like fans, saw-tooth shapes, or cubes, and so on. These images are from various sources and filed together by shape for use in future projects. She has trouble remembering names and book titles, but she always can find what she needs to know: "I am a great 'sorter outer.'" She says she is very good at finding out whatever is needed. She was pleased when she learned that Einstein once said something similar: He did not want to clutter his mind with things he could look up in a reference book. She likes to use both her right and left hands whenever possible, to keep both sides active.

From Carolyn's observations, I learned to see that the mind of a highly visual person is constantly playing with visual imagery in the world. The designer is constantly designing and redesigning.

DESIGN, COMPUTER GRAPHICS, AND DYSLEXIA— VALERIE DELAHAYE

Other forms of design are important for those working in the field of computer graphics, especially those making feature films. This is a new world in which strong visual thinkers, whether dyslexic or not, can find a place where their talents are greatly respected. One computer graphic artist, Valerie Delahaye, could not find work or be properly educated in France because of her dyslexia.[9] However, she found that she was warmly received by computer graphics companies in Canada and the United States. They were interested in her artistic and computer skills and thought her dyslexia was not a problem, especially since they already knew that many CG artists are dyslexic to some extent. In time, she had major responsibilities with many projects, including the feature films *The Fifth Element* and *Titanic*.

Delahaye estimates that about half of all computer graphics artists are probably dyslexic. Growing up in France, Valerie's difficulties with writing and working under pressure kept her from passing exams—even those required to enter art school. In the United States, however, she was able to benefit from testing accommodations so that she could receive a professional education in her areas of strength. She was not forced to be judged in areas that were largely irrelevant to her work and talent. She had expressed concern that the educational system in France still has done very little to address these problems and misconceptions relating to dyslexia.[10]

Her work experience is especially revealing. Valerie was 3-D manager at James Cameron's computer graphics effects company while working on *Titanic*. She was aware that many of the artists were dyslexic. She observed that the artists in her top group were unusually talented in their ability to come up with some of the most brilliant and advanced ways of visualizing whole scenes. They were able to accomplish the daunting task of creating the ship, the water, the sky, and human figures using only computer graphics. She observed that many dyslexics seem to be unusually talented in visualizing very complex scenes and ideas. Of course, this ability was extraordinarily useful in making the film *Titanic* because they had to re-create scenes that had never been photographed, as the only record was the oral reports given by survivors.

In hiring her team of top CG artists, Delahaye found that she had to pull videotapes out of the trash in the personnel office. The personnel staff would reject applicants based on their paper credentials and would not always bother to look at the videos. In contrast, Delahaye would never look at the written résumés. She looked only at the video samples of their work.

For example, she saw one tape in which the animation was poor but the lighting was great. So, she hired the individual who had done the lighting.

She also noted that the team members were easy to work with because they were so highly motivated. After so much failure in school, when given a chance, they wanted to show what they could really do. Also, they never had to read anything. When you are pushing the technology and the software to the limits, you cannot consult a manual or handbook. You have to ask your coworkers or work it out for yourself. It is an entirely oral culture—perfect for people with dyslexia. Those who are responsible for education and hiring need to understand that many of the old rules do not apply when you are on the edge of the really new.

TRANSFORMING OCCUPATIONS— NEW TECHNOLOGIES AND CLASSIC SKILLS

Delahaye's experience highlights for us the great changes that some occupations have been going through for some time—and the increasingly evident inconsistencies between the skills valued in the old verbal technological context and the skills highly valued in the emerging technologies of images and visualization. The old world of books and writing required one set of talents and skills, while the expanding world of moving images and visualized information seems to require quite a different set.

It would be wrong, however, to see these changes as relevant only to the graphic arts. Rather, there are good reasons to believe that the new technologies and techniques will, in time, spread to virtually all areas—from science and technology to all corners of business, education, and government. These technologies will provide a powerful set of new tools to analyze and manipulate all forms of information about ever more varied subject matter.

Some might argue that the move to images is quite superficial, as it would appear to shift attention and effort away from basic verbal literacy. However, a more persuasive argument can be made, especially for the young, that visual literacy will be as important, or possibly more important, then verbal literacy. Of course, it is desirable to have proficiency in both areas as much as possible. But we should not allow visual talent to be dropped by the wayside just because of verbal difficulties.

In addition, a case may be made that Delahaye's experience may be very close, indeed, to the experience of scientists and engineers generally. More and more, groups are coming to rediscover the importance of visual and spatial abilities—not only in art and design, but also in engineering, medicine, the sciences, mathematics, and related disciplines. Despite strong conventions of thought and common belief, we are seeing a gradual reawakening of interest in visual abilities that were formally thought to be relatively unimportant.

All forms of work are changing more rapidly and more extensively than most individuals and institutions are aware. Of course, we know that machines have taken over the tasks of many of the more routine functions of the copy editor, bank clerk, and bookkeeper. However, many are not aware that in similar fashion, it may not be very much longer before deep-learning computer systems and artificial-life agents learn to replicate reliably the more routine professional judgments of attorneys, engineers, physicians, and investment bankers.

Chapter Five

THOSE WHO CAN SEE

STUMBLING TOWARD THE TRUTH—THINKING LIKE A MARTIAN

Over and over again we have been focusing on stories about how our verbal culture fails because it is too fragmented, too limited, too specialized—while a visual, big-picture culture is ignored. We could see this as another example of the ancient Greek myth of Cassandra—who could see the future—but no one would believe her.

With many of those we have looked at, the pattern is clear: the new recognition of some big idea or concept; the battle against that new idea or concept by the conventional experts; the gradual recognition of the value of the key idea or concept—because over time it functions to reorganize lots of information or a whole field—and many apparently unrelated pieces fall into place. Eventually a new generation accepts the new vision as obvious and essential. The old believers fight a rearguard action in the courts and legislatures and (sometimes) universities, but the larger culture moves on, (almost fully) accepting as obvious the truth and usefulness of the new idea or concept. (Rarely, some special people, sometimes, make a reconciliation of the new with the old.)

In such times, and especially in our own, it can be quite useful to try to see the bigger picture by standing back a distance. In his book *Timescale: An Atlas of the Fourth Dimension*, the British science writer Nigel Calder writes of learning "how to be a Martian"—trying to learn how to see Earth and everything on it as it would be seen by a "dispassionate," disinterested, and distant being. Calder considers this exercise a way of identifying those things that are really important, the really substantial trends over time, which are often quite different from the presumed "serious business" of "pots, kings, and battles."[1]

Calder observes that it is quite difficult to cultivate this disinterested point of view. "Even the most skeptical historians," he notes, "seem barely able to distance themselves from the assumptions of their culture." Consequently, nearly "everyone takes it for granted that reading and writing are blessings." However, our education provides us with little awareness of the "high levels of sophistication" attained by non-literate peoples—who were nonetheless able to understand the stars and deep ocean currents well enough to navigate the broad Pacific, for example.

"Skill in archery," he observes, "may have been as important as writing in shaping the course of history." There is a great danger of seeing pre-literate or non-literate peoples as merely primitive and undeveloped. We are so well trained in the dominant values of our own culture that it is hard to give them due respect for their considerable accomplishments in the things that, after all, truly are most important in the face of great and continuous change and in the long history of human learning and survival.

We should not be surprised, Calder notes, that there is some self-promotion among the makers and users of books. In their own limited view, he says, schools measure the "worth of young citizens" based on their "facility in the cumbersome information technology displayed on the wafer of wood pulp in your hands." Our education institutions have given us little awareness that "most humans have lived and died unable to read or write, and some bright individuals are dyslexic." (This is a truly remarkable observation in passing—within a book that presumably has nothing to do with dyslexia or other learning differences. One wonders whether Calder and his famous father, Lord Ritchie Calder, have any personal experience with dyslexia, near or far. However, in my experience over many years, it is not at all unusual for such remarks to come from those scientists and writers working at very high levels, especially when dealing with big-picture issues.)

Driving the point home, Calder observes that "new technologies may soon make the art [of reading] as outmoded as oarsmanship for galleys." Consequently, he observes that the "emphasis laid upon literacy by scholars who earn their living with written words appears self-serving." In this way, if we take a very long view, then possibly we may begin to see the limitations of what we have been taught. Perhaps we may begin to see how even those who would appear to be the most educated could have special difficulty in seeing the kinds of trends that we are expecting.

Also, they may be so thoroughly entangled in the world of words, so "word bound," in fact, that they may be unable to perceive major changes just outside the boundary of their familiar world. (These prescient observations have greater impact today, when so many of us are now surrounded with small machines that can easily read to us, talk to us, fetch information for us, and translate languages for us—all at comparatively modest cost. This was previously unbelievable, even in science fiction, only a short time ago.)

The power and effectiveness of words, whether spoken or written, in whatever era or context, is not, of course, being challenged here. However, I do propose that the balance may be shifting (and may need to shift) in fundamental ways—that the important work of the world (the comparative advantage for some) will increasingly involve the sophisticated interpretation of complex images, using the newest technologies.

And, of course, we may very well see that we will have good reason to expect that the development of these new technologies and capabilities will be led by those creative visual thinkers (sometimes, or often, with learning difficulties or differences of some kind) who may have some special talent and experience in these areas. Consequently, we might anticipate not so much a shift from one style of thinking to another but rather a new balance between the two sides—that is, the restoration of a balance and interdependence between two modes of thought that has generally been rare (except among the most highly gifted)—one visual and one verbal. We might encounter (at a very different level) a new form of uncommon symmetry in thinking styles between the two hemispheres of the brain, which is still a major consideration, although unfashionable, in some circles these days.

Thus, it seems clear—taking the longer view—that some of the things that the best educated take for granted as permanent and enduring could actually be changing in fundamental ways. The "new technologies" that Calder talks about could very well be linked to the computer graphics, simulators, and information visualization that we have been talking about. If the trends move in the direction that I have been indicating, then some of the possible outcomes seem clear enough. When a new technology becomes widely available to amplify and extend some important human capacity, we may presume that it is only a matter of time before these potentials manifest in real consequences that will reverberate throughout our economy and culture.

A NEW CLASS OF MINDS

Calder's view is only one among a growing number of observers who have begun to see the deep implications of the coming changes. More individuals working at the edge of these new technological developments, in the sciences as well as in the professions or business, are beginning to recognize the emerging patterns.

One example is Dr. Larry Smarr, who is an astronomer, a physicist, the former director of the National Center for Supercomputing Applications, and the coauthor of a book called *Supercomputing and the Transformation of Science*. Over the years, Dr. Smarr came to see the likely impact of computer information visualization technologies and techniques. It is also notable that his observations include his perception of explicit connections between dyslexia and certain forms of creativity and high ability.

After we met at a computer graphics conference years ago, he sent me the following e-mail: "I have often argued in my public talks that the graduate education process that produces physicists is totally skewed to selecting those with analytic skills and rejecting those with visual or holistic skills. I have claimed that with the rise of scientific visualization as a new mode of scientific discovery, a new class of minds will arise as scientists. In my own life, my 'guru' in computational science was a dyslexic and he certainly saw the world in a different and much more effective manner than his colleagues. . . ."[2]

Smarr's perspective is especially worth noting because in many ways he and his colleagues have been working some decades years ahead of everyone else in the use of visualization technologies and related techniques. (They had supercomputing power before everyone else. Now nearly we all have on our desks machines as powerful as the early super computers, but few of us know how to use this power.) From this kind of perspective, it seems likely that we are indeed at the beginning of the major transition I have discussed previously.

Thus, we see that the outline of a new pattern has long been emerging. New technological tools have increasingly opened unexpected opportunities for new (or rediscovered) skills and talents. With the further development of smaller, cheaper, and progressively more powerful computers having sophisticated visualization and other capabilities, we should have expected long ago a new trend to emerge in which visual proficiencies would necessarily play an important role in areas that have been exclusively dominated in the past by those most proficient in verbal, logical, and mathematical modes of thought. While the use of these techniques has been expanding in the larger world, we are reminded that they have long been used, quietly and most effectively, in their own heads, by an extremely gifted few.

JAMES CLERK MAXWELL—WORKING IN WET CLAY

James Clerk Maxwell, as we have seen, acknowledged by many to be the most important physicist of the nineteenth century, knew how to be a supremely competent scientist and mathematician. Yet, when necessary, he could draw on the talents of the artist and sculptor—for he knew if he could find a way to "visualize the shape," then he could begin to really "understand" the vast complexity of the "system." When he wanted to understand some deep and complex pattern in nature, he often dismissed conventional analysis and notation. Instead, he used the visual and spatial tools of the craftsman, mechanic, and artist—modeling clay with wet hands to mold a tangible sculpture of the 3-D image in his mind's eye. According to a much later author: "If you can visualize the shape, you can understand the system."[3]

The fame of Maxwell's equations has meant that the name of James Clerk Maxwell is familiar to most persons having any form of scientific training. However, the full extent of his work and accomplishment is relatively little known. As early as 1860, Maxwell had begun the scientific study of color—and had projected the first color photograph. In addition to developing the electrodynamic theory of light, he also began the systematic application of statistical methods in physics, including original methods to explain the nature of Saturn's rings.

In 1868, he wrote the first important paper on the cybernetic and control theory so central to computer technology—through an analysis of the common spinning ball, or centrifugal, governor. Along with important contributions to the geometry of optics, he also developed certain mathematical terms and coined terminology related to the study of vectors (familiar to many as the arrows used to represent the direction and magnitude of a force).[4]

Maxwell's accomplishments were indeed remarkable. But it is also apparent that he had a number of the distinctive and mixed traits often seen in very strong visual thinkers. He seemed to have an unusual capacity to think in two ways: both visually and mathematically—and many of his considerable accomplishments may be traced to this ability. However, like many strong visual thinkers, Maxwell also had language difficulties.

On the one hand, he had no difficulty with reading or writing and was generally an excellent student for most of his life. However, on the other hand, he often struggled to collect his thoughts in order to answer an unexpected question on demand and under pressure. Additionally, he was a severe stutterer, and this continuing difficulty adversely affected his career as lecturer and professor.

As a child, he had shown a great love of drawing and had near relatives who were artists. He had a hearty and whimsical humor. And as an adult, he seemed to retain a childlike curiosity about everything, often recognizing similarities and making connections among the most diverse and apparently unrelated things.

GIBBS'S "GRAPHICAL METHOD"

An important illustration of the operation of Maxwell's visual-spatial thinking is his early appreciation of the work of the American physicist J.

Willard Gibbs, one of the major figures in the development of the study of thermodynamics. In the 1870s, Gibbs published a series of papers addressing the complex thermodynamic behavior of water and other fluids—using an unusual and innovative "graphical method," as he called it.

This method involved a three-dimensional mental model comparable to what we would now call a "surface plot"—a kind of 3-D graph that shows a number of points covering an undulating surface with rises and depressions like small mountains, hills, and valleys. As any point (representing a particular temperature, volume, pressure, etc.) moves over the surface plot, the conditions change in certain predictable ways, giving a deep understanding of the behavior of the complex system, based on being able to visualize the complex shape.

Gibbs wrote about his new method and described it mathematically, yet he made no effort to make a diagram of what was, apparently, clearly seen in his own mind's eye. The new method and the difficulty in having to visualize such complex material resulted in little attention from Gibbs's scientific colleagues, especially in the United States. Indeed, it is quite clear that Gibbs could see what others could not see.

MAXWELL'S SCULPTURED "FANCY SURFACE"

When Maxwell read Gibbs's papers in Britain, he immediately saw the power and the potential of the new graphical method that Gibbs had described mathematically. Indeed, so great was his interest that "he spent an entire winter" constructing a 3-D clay model of a surface using Gibbs's data.[5] As Maxwell explained in a letter to a scientist friend, "I have just finished a clay model of a fancy surface showing the solid, liquid, and gaseous states, and the continuity of the liquid and gaseous states."[6]

What Maxwell had made, then, was a kind of sculpture—patiently calculating the approximate position of each point in 3-D space and then adjusting the shape of the clay surface to correspond to the array of points in different positions (just as a sculptor or stone cutter would check his own work with a series of caliper measurements from an original model).

Maxwell sent a plaster of Paris cast of the clay model to Gibbs and kept two more in his own laboratory at Cambridge University. Gibbs's copy is still on display in a glass case outside of the Yale University Physics Department, while Maxwell's own copy remains on display at the new Cavendish Laboratory just outside Cambridge in England. Sculpture is a reproducible and durable medium, even in plaster.

What is most important for our discussion, then, is the way the highly visually oriented Maxwell immediately seized upon Gibbs's unusual but strikingly apt visual-spatial approach. Because Maxwell by this time was famous among scientists while Gibbs was entirely unknown, Maxwell was eventually able to move a whole generation of American and European scientists to appreciate the true value of Gibbs's novel approach.

However, while Gibbs's method and approach in mathematical form came to be fully appreciated over time, the visual and spatial model on which the method was based has been almost completely ignored for more than a century—until very recently. That is, for more than a century, Gibbs's equations have been memorized by students of nearly every technical occupation, yet the visualizations on which these equations are based received virtually no attention at all during this period.

REDISCOVERING THE GEOMETRY OF THERMODYNAMICS

As explained by University of Iowa chemistry professor Kenneth R. Jolls, "for those who could not follow the elaborate verbal manipulation of lines and planes in space that permeates [Gibbs's] writings, the physical meaning and the artistic beauty of these brilliant analogies were lost. Indeed, the interesting connections between thermodynamics and geometry, which were the essence of [Gibbs's] theoretical development, have all but vanished from the literature."[7]

Recently, however, with the development of computer-generated 3-D graphics, all of this has begun to change. Professor Jolls and his graduate student Daniel Coy developed a means of doing what Maxwell had done—but this time rapidly on a powerful graphics computer rather than over several months in modeling clay and plaster. According to Jolls, "there can be no doubt in the mind of any serious thermodynamicist" that images like those being produced on their computer screen "were vividly in [Gibbs's] mind as he wrote his famous trilogy [of papers] in the mid-1870s."[8]

So it is that the visual-thinking Maxwell immediately perceived the value of a visual-spatial approach that he could model in clay—but that we can now see modeled on a computer screen or in a virtual-reality display. The technology and the speed are enormously different, but the concept and the visual image in the mind's eye are exactly the same.

ANTICIPATING PIXAR AND THE
NATIONAL SCIENCE FOUNDATION

The reference to the art of sculpture is especially apt in the case of Maxwell. As I have noted in previous columns, strong family connections can often be observed between those with some form of dyslexia or learning disability and strong talents in the visual or performing arts. Also, it is commonly observed that many inventors have been artists or closely related to artists.

This connection is of particular interest to one of Maxwell's biographers as he attempts to gain a better understanding of Maxwell's extraordinary abilities: "The persistence of the artistic gift in a family so practical in outlook is a striking fact, one that must be born in mind in analyzing Maxwell's genius. Each generation threw up clever artists, among whom not the least able was Maxwell's cousin Jemima ... whose brilliant water-color paintings of Maxwell's childhood are a perpetual delight to Maxwell scholars."[9]

It is of perhaps no small import that the display case at the new Cavendish Laboratory outside Cambridge that holds Maxwell's plaster model also holds two zoetropes (rotating drums containing viewing slits) designed by Maxwell with images painted in watercolor with his own hand. One animation portrays a man and a woman dancing; the other animation displays two smoke rings interacting. Accordingly, we can easily say that in one glass case we have concrete evidence that Maxwell anticipated, with all else, the basics of the animated cartoon (brought to full computerized 3-D feature length by Pixar and Disney) as well as the first scientific visualization (long promoted at the Supercomputer Centers and elsewhere by the National Science Foundation).

MAXWELL "IN A PROP"

Maxwell's early biographers, Campbell and Garnett (1882), describe the period from 1847 to 1850, when Maxwell was between the ages sixteen and nineteen: "When he entered the University of Edinburgh, James Clerk Maxwell still occasioned some concern to the more conventional amongst his friends by the originality and simplicity of his ways. His replies in ordinary conversation were indirect and enigmatical, often uttered with hesitation and in a monotonous key...."

> When at table he often seemed abstracted from what was going on, being absorbed in observing the effects of refracted light in the finger-glasses, or in trying some experiment with his eyes—seeing round a corner, making invisible stereoscopes, and the like. Miss Cay [his aunt, the sister of his late mother] used to call attention by crying, "Jamsie, you're in a prop" [a mathematical proposition]. He never tasted wine; and he spoke to gentle and simple in exactly the same tone. On the other hand, his teachers...had formed the highest opinion of his intellectual originality and force....[10]

The brief description of Maxwell at the dinner table is particularly telling in establishing his relative disinterest in conventional table conversation and his persistent preoccupation with observing the operation of light and other natural phenomena, whatever the situation.

It is also notable that all these examples are of a visual nature ("trying some experiment with his eyes—seeing around a corner, making invisible stereoscopes"). These examples lend themselves to building mental models of optical interaction and spatial relationships, which are, in turn, closely related to the mathematics of area, field, line, and force.

Maxwell relied heavily upon visual, mechanical, and geometric approaches in his mathematical and scientific work. As one biographer observed: "Maxwell's starting point in mathematics was Euclidean geometry. Euclid is now so out of fashion that few people know the excitement of his intellectual rigor.... With Maxwell the love of geometry stayed. ... The love of geometry also helped interest Maxwell in Faraday's ideas about lines of force."[11]

The common thread throughout the great variety of Maxwell's accomplishments is the interplay of force and substance in a largely visual-spatial arena. The visual-spatial dominated his work. However, from the stories of his daily life we might also infer that he was thinking in geometric terms much of the time, wherever he was and whatever he was doing.

SHIFTING PERSPECTIVES—WAYS OF SEEING

Maxwell's writing and research show an unusual flexibility of mind, which seems to be characteristic of some strong visual thinkers. Maxwell could move from one structure to another quite different structure with relative ease, retaining underlying similarities of approach. "Maxwell . . . was continually changing his outlook. His five leading papers on electromagnetic theory written between 1855 and 1868 each presented a complete view of the subject, and each viewed it from a different angle. It is this variety that makes Maxwell's writings, in Jeans's words, a kind of enchanted fairyland: one never knows what to expect next."[12]

Maxwell was a professional scientist, but he was able to see well beyond the conventional science of his day. He was as fully at home in the intuitive and visual world as he was with the world of the "professed mathematicians." He knew mathematics, but he did not think in the same way as the conventional mathematicians of his time. He knew their ways but was not restricted by them.

He approached physical phenomena with complex mechanical models, yet when he was finished, all such analogies were made impossible by his mathematics (at least for a time). The consequences of his work were so extensive and profound that they set the research agenda for the next half century. Yet, he never received, during his lifetime, the recognition given his contemporaries of lesser stature.

Maxwell was well educated, but his career was only modestly successful. His speech difficulties limited his professional advancement throughout his life. Although he was eventually appointed head of the new Cavendish Laboratory at Cambridge University, it was only after two other preferred candidates had declined the position.

Sadly, he died too young to elaborate his work fully or to gain full recognition for his accomplishments. Yet in the physical sciences his work came to be acknowledged as the most important product of the entire nineteenth century. Maxwell never was able to lecture well, but he taught generations, sometimes because he was willing to renounce troublesome words and notation and attempt to visualize complex patterns in nature by molding wet clay with bare hands.

WHY ARE SOME OF THE BEST WRITERS DYSLEXIC?

As we have seen, some of the best scientists are successful because they are strong visual thinkers. Strangely, I would argue that some of the best writers are successful, in part, for the same reason.

A few years ago, I was asked to contribute a short piece for a new book, an anthology of prose and poetry by dyslexic writers, to be published in the United Kingdom by a group called RASP. Later, the editor, Naomi Folb, asked if I would be willing to write a foreword for the volume as well. I was delighted to do it—and I was even more delighted because the whole argument came tumbling out with no apparent effort on my part. (I wish this would happen more often. Normally, I have to struggle to find the right words, redrafting often.) I was also pleased when I saw the finished book with the following quotation of mine standing alone on the inside front cover: "The truth-talking commentator who is not caught up in the race. They have felt the otherness from the start."[13]

My argument in the foreword went as follows:

There are many puzzles and paradoxes linked to dyslexia. One of the most strange of these is that some of the best writers are dyslexic. How can this be so? How can those who struggle so with words become such masters of words? Well, good writing is different from good spelling, reading out loud or rapid recall of memorized texts.

Good writing often requires an ear for the sound of language.

Good writing often requires a strong visual imagination with powerful images and metaphors communicated through the words. Often the best writing is very plain, using well the most simple language. Also, good writing requires fresh language—not the usual string of conventional terms and syntax. Good writing is thoughtful and sometimes surprising in its content and form.

Oddly, the difficulties experienced by dyslexics sometimes can lead directly to becoming advantages in service of the best writing. Dyslexics are a heterogeneous group. They are unlike non-dyslexics. They are unlike each other. But there are many common elements. They often, almost by definition, learn to read late and very slowly (after a long and difficult struggle). This is partly the reason that many never lose the sound of language in their head—as happens with rapid and efficient readers.

They often have powerful visual imaginations—seeing pictures in their minds as they read or speak. Some of the best storytellers say they never remember the words of a story. Rather, they have a movie running in their head and they simply talk about what they see. You don't have to be dyslexic to do this. But dyslexics seem inclined to do this—whether they want to or not. But as one can readily see, if you cannot remember texts as texts—but only see images—then the words are likely to be different each time. Sometimes fresh. Sometimes surprising. Sometimes shockingly apt.

Often I have heard the phrase, "they see what others don't see or cannot see." I have heard the phrase a thousand times, in a thousand different settings. It is not only having strong powers of observation. There is something going on in these larger than usual, slow moving, apparently overly-connected brains that yields perceptions and insights often denied to non-dyslexics—who may see the unexpected connection when they are shown. But they would never see it on their own.

Some say dyslexics are prone to ponder. Non-dyslexics may have a look, see what they have been taught to see, say the expected words and quickly move on—scoring high on conventional tests of conventional observations. (This drives artists crazy. So many of the clever students learn the words to say about a painting and then they think they understand it. But they never learn to really see it.)

Many dyslexics find it very difficult to do things automatically—which can be a problem. It can be very slow. Whether training the movements of their body (as in an Olympic sport) or observing nature (in a literary or scientific puzzle), they have to think and think hard. Big brains with many connections move slowly—but they can do jobs that fast smaller brains cannot do. They see the big picture. They see connections between apparently unrelated things.

Those who ponder hold on to an idea or problem or puzzle for a long time, turning it over and over. In literature, sometimes they come up with a fresh and deep insight. (In science or technology, sometimes they come up with a remarkable and unexpected discovery.)

It is a commonplace that the best artist or writer is an outsider, observing human events at the edge. Again, many non-dyslexics can take on this role. But many dyslexics, because of their deep humiliations from the earliest days, seem naturally to assume the role of distant observer. The truth-talking commentator who is not caught up in the race. They have felt the otherness from the start.

In my own research on talents among highly successful dyslexics, my literary friends were shocked and disbelieving when I told them that the most severely dyslexic historical person I came across was the Irish poet William Butler Yeats. It teaches us. Even in times unfriendly to formal poetry, his lines show up in songs and commentaries and book titles. He said that he often started with a rhythm, a pulse, and the sense then followed. He never lost the feeling of the sound of the language.

And everywhere you look there are vivid metaphors and images. About his early life, Yeats says: "I was unfitted for school work. . . . My thoughts were a great excitement, but when I tried to do anything with them, it was like trying to pack a [large hot air] balloon in a shed in a high wind." A few years before his death, he observed: "It was a curious experience . . . to have an infirm body and an intellect more alive than it had ever been, one poem leading to another as if . . . lighting one cigarette from another."[14]

I closed the foreword with these words: "I am honored to introduce this volume of the work of dyslexic writers—sometimes harsh and angry, sometimes as beautiful as a song, sometimes so short and powerful that you feel you have been punched with a boxer blow. But always fresh, truth telling, full of vivid and unexpected sounds and images."

Chapter Six

INSIDERS, OUTSIDERS

> Primates are visual animals. No other group of mammals
> relies so strongly on sight. Our attraction to images as
> a source of understanding is both primal and pervasive.
> Writing, with its linear sequencing of ideas, is a histor-
> ical afterthought in the history of human cognition.
>
> —Steven Jay Gould

The above are the observations of the naturalist and essayist Stephen Jay Gould, who asserts that it is quite remarkable that words occupy such an extraordinarily important position in human culture, when in fact we are by nature highly visual. He notes, however, that "traditional scholarship has lost this root to our past. Most research is reported by text alone, particularly in the humanities and social sciences."[1] He observes that "pictures, if included at all, are poorly reproduced, gathered in a center section divorced from relevant text, and treated as little more than decoration."

Gould touches on a matter that is one of the central themes developed in this book, as well as of my previous writings and talks. I have made an effort to investigate the deep tension in the ways human beings and human brains handle information about the world. While the process is in reality highly complex, I have found it useful to distinguish between verbal and visual approaches to knowledge or style of thought. These two common terms seem to effectively categorize the root differences between the analytical and sequential modes thinking in contrast to the global and simultaneous modes of thought. These styles of thinking also seem to be reflected broadly in institutions, occupations, and cultural trends.

In recent intellectual history, there has been a lack of balance between the verbal and visual approaches. We have been taught to believe that to think clearly about something, it has to be done in words (or perhaps even the lessor known special symbols of mathematics or formal logic). As we have seen, many deny that it is really useful or even possible to think in pictures. For the more extreme adherents of this point of view, diagrams and images may be seen as useful for explaining ideas to ordinary people, but they are to be avoided at all costs by serious professionals.

Such beliefs have long been evident in Western culture—varying from field to field and from time to time—for hundreds of years. With a few exceptions, the highest prestige has been associated with positions that are connected with written language and the book—for the clerks and priests who had proximity to power, for the members of the small elite who had a proper academic education and gained much of their status and authority from full control over the technology of making and using books. It seems possible, however, that now much of this might be changing in fundamental ways. With new and powerful technological developments, a new form of elite may be slowly taking shape—unnoticed, mammal-like, going about their own business at the feet of giants.

Thus, as I have tried to argue in *In the Mind's Eye*, it may be that we are now at a turning point where a new family of relatively inexpensive and powerful visually oriented technologies is making it possible to complement the long-effective use of verbally oriented technologies. And as this transition takes place, if my speculations and expectations are correct, we may come to better understand the other kinds of "smartness" exhibited by the visually talented—individuals who have often, in the past, been recognized not by their talents but by their puzzling but persistent difficulties with words.

With the new visual technologies and techniques, we may find that some of those who struggled most with the old system of words may be just the ones who will move ahead most rapidly in the cutting-edge system of images, where so much that is really new is still beginning to be formed. We can now see the first broad and serious consideration of "visual literacy" (in some cases linked to "digital literacy") such that there is a growing awareness that proficiency with words or even numbers is not enough, at any level—that new forms of basics need to be mastered by nearly everyone—but that these new basics are quite different from reading, writing, and arithmetic. However, as we approach this very new situation, it is perhaps some comfort to realize that concerns about the effects of technological change are not really unheard-of.

SINGAPORE'S ELDER STATESMAN—LEE KUAN YEW

For several years I had hoped to find historical or contemporary examples of highly respected individuals from non-Western cultures who would fit the larger patterns of high ability with some form of learning problems. In Western cultures, it is difficult enough to discuss things that are perceived as possible defects—especially among men, who typically learn early the possible costs of showing signs of weakness that might be exploited by others.[2] As difficult as these discussions are in Western groups, it appears that they are actually much more difficult in Asian and Middle Eastern groups. Foreign students who are tested for dyslexia and learning disabilities in American universities, for example, seem to have an unusually difficult time getting past their denial, because they perceive it as a social stigma that seems to be much more severe than that experienced by many Westerners. For these reasons, I was especially delighted to discover that a series of newspaper articles in Hong Kong and Singapore had announced early in 1996, in no uncertain terms, that Lee Kuan Yew, perhaps the most respected senior statesman throughout all of Asia, had revealed that he had "mild dyslexia." His story is briefly told in the first pages of a recent book published by the Dyslexia Association of Singapore.[3] Lee's daughter, Dr. Lee Wei Ling, had learned of her own dyslexia as part of her medical training in Boston and realized that her father seemed to have similar problems—so she suggested that her father be tested. These revelations were made as part of an announcement that royalties for a new CD-ROM of Lee Kuan Yew's life would be donated to the Dyslexia Association of Singapore. The association chairman noted that when Senior Minister Lee revealed that he had mild dyslexia, a major stigma was removed and parents were willing to have their children tested. Clearly, Lee Kuan Yew's revelations could have continuing positive effects beyond Singapore—as they also make us wonder at what possible connections his dyslexia may have with his visionary and long-standing political leadership. It is no small matter that Singapore, long a leader in technological and commercial innovation, has become a leader in the effort to take advantage of the distinctive talents of dyslexic children and adults. In November 2014, the Dyslexia Association of Singapore launched a program called "Embrace Dyslexia." (It happens that this writer was asked to travel to Singapore in November 2014 to give five talks as part of the kickoff for this program.)

ENGINEERING BY HAND AND EYE

In his book *Engineering and the Mind's Eye*, Eugene Ferguson provides an overview of developments in engineering education and practice over long periods and in recent times, providing an assessment of some of the larger implications and consequences of progressively abandoning visual and nonverbal approaches. While there has been no specific reference to dyslexia, this book on long-term trends in engineering education has argued that an excessive concern with esoteric mathematical approaches has altered the field, driving out visually oriented, practical, hands-on engineers—generally weakening the field and increasing problems from complex systems because too many practitioners are trained to do their specialty but none are trained to look at the complex whole. His observations are clearly consistent with the problems that I have been discussing here:

> Until the 1960s, a student in an American engineering school was expected by his teachers to use his mind's eye to examine things that engineers had designed—to look at them, listen to them, walk around them, and thus to develop an intuitive "feel" for the way the material world works (and sometimes doesn't work).... By the 1980s, engineering curricula had shifted to analytical approaches, so that visual and other sensual knowledge of the world seemed much less relevant.... As faculties dropped drawing and shop practice from their curricula and deemed plant visits unnecessary, ... working knowledge of the material world disappeared from faculty agendas and therefore from student agendas, and the nonverbal, tacit, and intuitive understanding essential to engineering design atrophied.[4]

DOING MATH INSTEAD OF WATCHING MATH—JERRY UHL

In the past, what is now often called scientific visualization was rare in many fields. This is changing. As we have seen, in the past few years, the world of the professional mathematician has been undergoing fundamental change—reversing, in many respects, more than a hundred years of development in the opposite direction. In recent years, professional mathematicians have been rethinking the way that they view their whole discipline—as well as the ways they think their discipline should be taught. In the old days (not very long ago), logic and rigorous proof were seen as the most important aspects of serious mathematics. In recent years, however, this has changed. Currently, many leading professional mathematicians now see that visualization, experimentation, and original discovery are of prime importance—a position unthinkable by most respectable mathematicians only a short time ago.[5]

An emerging consensus point of view has been described by one mathematics professor who is familiar with years of debate within the profession:

> Mathematics is often defined as the science of space and number, as the discipline rooted in geometry and arithmetic. Although the diversity of modern mathematics has always exceeded this definition, it was not until the recent resonance of computers and mathematics that a more apt definition became fully evident. Mathematics is the science of patterns. The mathematician seeks patterns in number, in space, in science, in computers, and in imagination. . . . To the extent that mathematics is the science of patterns, computers change not so much the nature of the discipline as its scale: computers are to mathematics what telescopes and microscopes are to science. . . . Because of computers, we see that mathematical discovery is like scientific discovery. . . . Theories emerge as patterns of patterns, and significance is measured by the degree to which patterns in one area link to patterns in other areas. . . .[6]

The far-reaching consequences of this change in perspective can be partly seen in the concurrent major reevaluation of certain university-level mathematics courses in recent years. Although this reevaluation has been widespread—with many alternative proposals for improvements and extensive debate among professional mathematicians—in most instances real change has been slow to take place. And in many cases those changes actually implemented have been relatively modest in scope.

In some cases, on the other hand, the changes have been quite extensive, with dramatic results. For example, three professors have developed innovative courseware for teaching calculus as an interactive laboratory course using a graphics computer together with a high-level mathematics program—one designed to do mathematics in all of its three major forms: numerical, symbolic, and graphical.

Unlike many other course innovations, such changes are not just additions to the regular class lectures, but rather, they have had enormous impact in transforming all aspects of the teaching and learning process. Instead of spending lots of time learning by hand routines that can be quickly done by the computer, the students are pressed to move rapidly on to high-level conceptual matters and a variety of practical problems, focusing mainly on examples from medicine, biology, and the life sciences. This is in marked contrast to the traditional calculus problem sets that are now seen by professional mathematicians in Europe as well as America as being highly contrived and artificial, with little relevance to real mathematics in either research or application.

A recent unpublished evaluation summarizes some of the radical curricular innovations and the increased effectiveness of this new type of laboratory calculus course:

> The [new] course changed the delivery of calculus from lectures and texts to a laboratory course through an electronic interactive text.... One of the most remarkable characteristics was [the students'] exploration through calculation and plottings. In the traditional calculus courses, the instructor announces the mathematical theory and then reinforces it with examples and exercises, and students recite the theory and solve problems illustrating the theory. [In the new course], however, the learning pattern of students ... was dramatically different. The experimentation by redoing, reformatting, rethinking, adapting, and making changes led students to discover the basic concepts and

principles [for themselves]. . . . The students . . . indicated that they had a feel for "doing" mathematics instead of "watching" mathematics. . . .[7]

As we try to identify the causes of success in this approach, it may be no small matter that the students are encouraged to think and learn visually first—before traditional lectures and verbal description. A major shift in learning technique (along with a delightful informality and irreverence) is apparent in the authors' explanation to their students:

One of the beauties of learning the CALCULUS&*Mathematica* way is your opportunity to learn through graphics you can interact with. *In this course, your eyes will send ideas directly to your brain.* And this will happen without the distraction of translating what your eyes see into words. Take advantage of this opportunity to learn visually with pure thought uncorrupted by strange words. The words go onto an idea only after the idea has already settled in your mind. This aspect of CALCULUS&*Mathematica* distinguishes it from other math courses.[8]

It is perhaps also of no small importance that students who learn in this new way have shown that, in comparison with the traditional course, they understand the basic concepts better, can remember the information longer, and can apply the concepts to practical uses more effectively. It is increasingly apparent that many of the consequences seen in this new teaching approach—using interactive graphical computer systems with advanced software and courseware—may indicate possibilities for effective innovation in many other disciplines. Thus, these new teaching approaches may be merely one manifestation of a much larger trend as many disciplines find distinctive ways to return to visual thinking and learning.

STORIES AS A BETTER DIAGNOSTIC TOOL

Several years ago, after giving a talk in Santa Barbara, I met a child and adolescent psychiatrist who said he had been using *In the Mind's Eye* as a diagnostic tool for years. He explained that he had given his clients something like forty or fifty copies so far. He asked them to highlight in yellow all those traits that were like themselves and cross out all those that were unlike themselves. I said, "Oh, you mean the list at the end of the book." He said, "Oh no, I use the whole book—it is much more useful than the usual tests and measures. They are all devised by linear thinkers for linear thinkers." Afterward, it occurred to me that the whole book indeed could readily serve as a rambling catalogue of traits—but that it also would not hurt that these clients would be forced to see in themselves traits shared by important persons who accomplished a great deal, sometimes in spite of their difficulties but more often *because* of their difficulties and their very different ways of thinking.

To succeed with such extremely mixed abilities, as these individuals often do, you need to have a deep reservoir of confidence and fortitude to carry on in spite of the judgments of others that you are, in fact, really slow and lazy and stupid.

To maintain the required drive, determination, and sense of mission in the face of almost constant early failure and humiliation is often nothing short of miraculous. It would appear that only a comparatively small number survive these early days with enough confidence and drive to press on, against all odds, to find success in some area of special knowledge, deep understanding, and passionate interest.

Much of *In the Mind's Eye* was an attempt to understand the nature of this kind of success and the remarkable individuals who seem able to find their way around so many obstacles, seeking an area in which they are at home with their work, often performing at very high levels of proficiency and productivity.

I have come to believe that those of us who are trying to understand and to help dyslexics (along with others more or less like them) must come to see that conventional academic remediation is only part of the job—and not the most interesting or important part.

We need to seek ways to help dyslexics find and develop their own talents, large or small, so that they cannot be beaten down—pushed into hiding their talents along with their disabilities. I, for one, believe that one of the best ways—perhaps the only truly effective way—to do this is to study the lives and work of highly successful dyslexics (in some detail and in all of their great diversity), so as to allow other dyslexics to see what can be done and to show how it can be done.

SEEING MORE IN AN IMAGE THAN OTHERS— BERYL BENACERRAF

Beryl Benacerraf, MD, is a world-renowned radiologist and a pioneer in the use of ultrasound. Her specialty is interpreting ultrasound images in the care of fetuses. She is also dyslexic—and she has been willing to share her experience of her struggles coupled with her high visual abilities. "Because of dyslexia," she says, "my brain works differently, and I can see these patterns. I do have a gift that other people don't have, and I will always stay ahead of the crowd and see more in an image than other people."[9]

In her early education, reading was very difficult, but she could see patterns. During reading instruction she found ways to hide her inabilities. She knew she wouldn't be able to read the paragraph out loud on demand when called upon. She could not work out the words and read that fast. And she couldn't tell anyone, because they would think she was stupid. But she could see a way out. She counted classmates, and counted the paragraphs. She found the paragraph she would be called upon to read. She struggled over and over to read it—memorizing it—making each word her own, until when the time came she could lift her head and recite it.

In her work, this ability to see patterns allowed Dr. Benacerraf to notice an unusual fold of skin on the necks of some of the unborn babies. No one had noticed it before. It was only later that she and her colleagues realized that the children with the extra fold of skin suffered from Down syndrome. The fold was a sign of the syndrome, and it could be seen during the pregnancy.

However, other physicians were skeptical. When she wrote papers about her findings, other physicians thought she was wrong. "I was booed off the stage. 'Who is this crazy person talking about the neck fold?'" Her findings were controversial for a very long time, and she was denied admittance to radiological societies on account of it. But she wanted an academic career, so she persevered. Gradually, the other physicians came to realize that she was right.

Long before she knew she was dyslexic, Beryl was coming up with adaptive strategies to avoid problems. She applied for early decision to Barnard, thus avoiding standardized tests until after she was admitted. She used her native French to satisfy the language requirement. Her studies in science allowed her to avoid taking history. She was able to dictate her papers to classmates who were happy to type them up. Being from a family of creative and successful people instilled within her a native confidence—and, she acknowledged, it helped to have a Nobel Prize winner as a father when she applied for medical school.[10]

But once she was in medical school, it was clear that she belonged. Her professor, a senior radiologist at Massachusetts General Hospital, told her, "I've never seen anybody with your ability in the thirty years that I've been practicing." Benacerraf looked at other specialties, but she saw that her ability to see patterns was a real strength in one area: "Radiology is where I belonged. I live in a world of patterns and images and I see things that no one else sees. Anomalies jump out at me like a neon sign."

AN UNBELIEVABLE DISCOVERY AND
AN OPENED DOOR—MARY SCHWEITZER

Mary had hardly slept for weeks. She was sure that no one would believe her. Maybe there was some mistake. She had checked and rechecked—but she found the same results. Mary had seen things that no one had ever seen before. She had seen the calcium deposits inside the fossil bone—the deposits normally stored within bird bones to provide calcium for the eggshells to be produced by a pregnant female.

But then she also saw the tiny flexible blood vessels and remnant red blood cells. All of this would not have been surprising for any biologist or ornithologist observing a modern bird. But this was not just any bird. This was the fossilized femur of a pregnant *Tyrannosaurus rex*—a bone that was 68 million years old—a bone that had once belonged to a kind of bird that had originally weighed tons.[11]

Fossil bones are precious. No one had ever cut one in half. No one had ever thought that there would be anything of interest inside. No one would have guessed that tiny blood vessels, red blood cell remnants, and intact protein fragments might be there. This was impossible. There was no way for such things to be preserved for so long. It was clearly not possible. Everybody knew it. Yet, there it was.

Mary Higby Schweitzer, a former student of Jack Horner, had trained as a biologist before she studied paleontology. Most people in the field had studied geology—the rocks within which the bones were buried. Few had studied the biology of the living animals buried inside the rocks. Accordingly, Mary could easily recognize the calcium deposits inside the bone, in the medullary cavity.

Of course, it was partly a fortunate accident. In this case, the fossil bone had been found in a very remote part of the badlands of Montana. There was no road. The grad students had to walk in and work hard to remove the rock above the fossil. Once uncovered, the bone had to be encased in plaster to protect it during transportation. But the whole mass was too heavy for the loaned helicopter to lift it. So it had to be cut in half. The cut was clean. Often fossil bones are painted with chemicals and clear coats to protect them from further decay. But these would introduce modern substances that would contaminate the fossil, especially at the molecular level. Mary had been given a clean specimen, entirely free of modern contamination.

Once it was made public, Mary's discovery was not believed by many professionals in the field. Biochemists and paleontologists greeted her work with "howls of skepticism."[12] They could not believe that organic molecules "could survive for tens of millions of years." So Schweitzer and her postdoc, Elena Schroeter, repeated their investigations with extreme care to avoid any possibility of contamination.

Very recently (February 2017), their new investigations were published—and they are now believed. One expert, who had been skeptical before, called Schweitzer's recent paper a "milestone" and said he is now "fully convinced beyond a reasonable doubt the evidence is authentic." Now that they have shown that ancient molecules can survive over very long time periods, a new path to scientific investigation has emerged—"to pin down the evolutionary relationships among different dinosaurs, as well as among ancient mammals and other extinct creatures." The *Science* magazine article concludes, "Says Schweitzer: 'The door is now open.'"

The story of Mary Schweitzer's discoveries and persistence provides us with a wonderful example of how major new information can come from seeing things differently, asking basic questions never asked before, taking risks and recognizing something unexpected, seeing something that others could not see—seeing something that could have been recognized by others. But they did not see it. It was Mary who saw what others could not see—or would not see.

Chapter Seven

SEEING AND TECHNOLOGY

MISGIVINGS ABOUT A NEW TECHNOLOGY

Some time ago, a well-known social critic described a number of misgivings he had about a new technology that threatened to revolutionize the society that he knew, dramatically changing interpersonal relationships as it devalued direct human contact, forever changing communication, work, and the educational process.

Commentary such as this is familiar to us today, everywhere, but we should not be entirely surprised to find that this particular social critic was Plato's Socrates—and that the dangerous and destructive technology he was talking about is in fact the book. Socrates explained that this new technology has several weaknesses. It is artificial and, unlike a living person, it is inflexible and insensitive to its listener and its surroundings.

It is unable to adjust what it is saying to what would be appropriate for certain listeners or specific times or places. The book could not be properly interactive, as in a conversation or a dialogue with real people, with disagreements and multiple points of view. And, finally, according to Socrates, with a book the written words "seem to talk to you as if they were intelligent, but if you ask them anything about what they say, from a desire to be instructed, they go on telling you just the same thing forever."[1]

After more than two millennia, it now seems that a new kind of technology, with interactive multimedia capabilities, may be beginning to address some of Socrates's main concerns. As we move forward into what seems like unknown territory, we might find it useful to measure the degree of our modern success by his ancient standard. Coming full circle, then, we can now see that we should ask our new technologies to behave less like a book and more like a responsive, sensitive, and intelligent human being.

Each new technology, if powerful and productive, of necessity will create new things as it will be destructive to older things. It is also likely that each truly new technology—as it comes to be used in effective ways in many spheres of education, work, and life—will gradually but unalterably change some of our basic mental furniture, including our ideas about talent and intelligence, our ideas about what is worth knowing and what is worth doing. As we have seen before, this is one of the central lessons learned from Dr. Norman Geschwind.

We have not been trained to see the world this way. We have been schooled to think of talent and intelligence as more or less absolute and unchanging—not as something dependent on variable intellectual fashions or on the kinds of technologies that are thought to be important at one time or another. Yet, as we have seen through the course of this book and the profiles I offer in *In the Mind's Eye*, highly talented people can sometimes have great difficulties because their mix of strengths and weaknesses do not exactly correspond to those desired by the dominant culture at a certain time—although they may eventually prove, somewhat later, to be just what is wanted. In a culture dominated mainly by words, visual talents often are viewed as merely incidental and ancillary. But as new visual technologies show their true power, we may expect perceptions of value to change in dramatic ways, perhaps leaning away from the verbal and toward the visual.

Thus, the continuing prestige of the written word, we can now see, is wrapped up in the power of the book as a technology. As Socrates saw, this technology, for all its great and obvious advantages, created barriers against easy human interaction and dialogue. It changed forever the transitory and ephemeral nature of ordinary speech—as it destroyed forever the long-standing and honorable oral tradition. In a similar fashion, we may expect the new technology of computer graphics and data visualization to deeply transform our own culture. We may expect a gradual shift from a world in which "serious" work is based largely on words to a new world in which images will have an increasingly powerful role.

In this new world, if our expectations are correct, the real action will be in teaching ourselves how to use the rich, multidimensional channels of simultaneous and nonsequential information inherent in these new technologies—using these channels to develop deep and sophisticated understandings of highly complex systems in ways never before possible. For a long time our science has advanced largely by reducing the complex to the simple. But not all things are amenable to this strategy; and sometimes having an understanding of the complex big picture is integral or a prerequisite to understanding the simplified aspects of the concept or idea at hand. Now, with these new visual technologies, we may have the ability to investigate and consider complex things as complex things. And we may expect that often this will be done by internalizing highly complex moving images—by linking new technologies with newly discovered talents—by building mental models in the mind's eye. However, when we are trying to get a handle on substantial change such as this, sometimes it is useful to take a much longer and larger view.

THE DRAWING MACHINE—BENOIT MANDELBROT

Benoit Mandelbrot has come to be recognized as one of the giants in the development of new mathematical theory. He invented the word *fractal* for "fractal dimension," the concept that lies behind the mathematics and images associated with his name. His work challenges our concepts of mathematics. We are accustomed to drawing in two dimensions and doing sculpture in three dimensions; but how can we can we conceive of doing anything in 2.5 dimensions, or, worse, in 0.63 dimensions? Mandelbrot's book *The Fractal Geometry of Nature*, full of fascinating images and ideas, is acknowledged to be one of the major works in the field. Remarkably, it has also sold more copies than any other book of higher mathematics, a surprisingly popular bestseller of an unusual sort.[2]

For a long time, Mandelbrot, like many other pioneers, worked in comparative obscurity and largely alone, covertly following his interest in a variety of fields he had never studied (economics, engineering, medicine, etc.) as experts looked on with suspicion. "He was always an outsider, taking an unorthodox approach to an unfashionable corner of mathematics, exploring disciplines in which he was rarely welcomed, hiding his grandest ideas in efforts to get his papers published, surviving mainly on the confidence of his employers."[3]

Mandelbrot's way of working, we should not be surprised to discover, is described as intensely intuitive and visual. His early education was interrupted because he was hiding from the Nazis in the countryside of occupied France. When he had to take exams to enter university, Mandelbrot found that he could usually hide his lack of training by relying on his geometrical intuition.

A self-avowed "nomad by choice" and "pioneer by necessity," Mandelbrot worked under the shelter of IBM's Thomas J. Watson Research Center, journeying over some thirty years from "obscurity to eminence" but never really finding a true intellectual home. Clearly, Mandelbrot is one of the strong visual thinkers in which we are most interested. It is also likely that he exhibited dyslexic traits to some extent.

Indeed, I met Dr. Mandelbrot at a three-day MIT conference to which I was invited. I had wondered whether I would have an opportunity to talk to him. But as it happens, it was a small meeting and most of the speakers and attendees stayed all three days. Consequently, we had several conversations. At one point, I asked him if he had ever seen dyslexia among his mathematical colleagues. He laughed and said, "if you ask my wife, she is convinced that I am dyslexic." I also heard later from other sources that he talked about his dyslexia in other settings. We need not make a big case of whether someone is actually properly diagnosed as dyslexic according to some particular definition. Rather, I believe that what we really need to look at is the apparent trade-off between certain difficulties that are associated with extreme visual proficiencies of some kind.

Sometimes it's revealing to look at the early life experience these individuals. In one set of interviews, Mandelbrot gave details about his early life and education. I will quote some of this below. This passage, I think, gives us an insight into how Mandelbrot came to his major discoveries using computer graphics.

I had absolutely no experience in drawing. There was no temptation. My father was very much interested in painting, and I remember very well the first day when we arrived in Paris, after the first weekend, when he found he had time to walk and take us around Paris. He took us to the Louvre and to the Conservatory of Arts and Crafts, which is a museum where they keep old planes, old cars, and so on, because he wanted us to know about technology. He was very, very keen on that, and he also wanted to share his love of classical painting, in particular the art of Titian. But I didn't know that I could draw; but at that time, during the preparation for the École Normale [Supérieure] and the École Polytechnique, . . . drawing was just part of the program. It sounded ridiculous because there was no need for it, but again it was a tradition. Once upon a time, engineers had to be able to draw the state of something happening for their bosses, or, if they're coming to inspect a bridge being built, to draw what was happening. Therefore, drawing was an important part of the game, and to train that skill in a kind that could be also subjected to exams, we had—well, the *Venus de Milo*, the [*Winged*] *Victory of Samothrace*, the head of Voltaire, etc., etc.—all kinds of classical and French sculptures to imitate. And I found that I could do it very accurately. It was rather soulless but extremely accurate and extremely careful depiction. All that was part of this complex of skills, which, again, amazingly enough, I did not know about before, namely the ability to draw, to see things in accurate detail, to see differences between my drawing and the model very accurately, and to think in terms of pictures. I might say that this has been my skill throughout, that in all the very complicated ups and downs of my life, the ability to think globally, in certain configurations, has been predominant. The ability, the willingness, to ask myself questions about what shapes things are, because then I could think about them, has been predominant. In my work in pure mathematics, most of it—the parts most exciting for mathematicians—has been parts in which I was asking questions which nobody else had asked before, because nobody else had actually looked at certain structures in that manner. Therefore, as I will tell, the advent of the computer, not as a computer but as a drawing machine, was for me a major event in my life. That's why I was motivated to participate in the birth of computer graphics, because for me computer graphics was a way of extending my hand, extending it and being able to draw things which my hands, myself, and the hands of nobody else before, would not have been able to represent.[4]

Here Mandelbrot's words clearly foreshadow his later line of substantial discovery. As he says, "I was asking questions which nobody else and asked before, because nobody else had actually looked at certain structures in that manner." Clearly, Mandelbrot was seeing things that other people could not see or would see.

WITH MANDELBROT ON WALL STREET AND IN YOUR POCKET

Even when I thought I was somewhat familiar with Mandelbrot's impact on computer graphics and formal mathematics (as well as some aspects of popular culture and design), I found myself to be quite surprised at several unexpected additional connections—connections that were not small.

A while back, I was trying to understand what had happened to Wall Street in 2007–2008. I was reading a book by *Wall Street Journal* reporter Scott Patterson, *The Quants—How a New Breed of Math Whizzes Conquered Wall Street and Nearly Destroyed It*. The mathematicians seemed to have found a way to understand patterns in the market and how to make money from it—for a while. But then it all came crashing down. I was especially struck by a passage describing the events of August 6, 2007:

That Monday afternoon...something was going wrong.... The stocks its models picked to buy and sell were moving in strange directions—directions that meant huge losses.... The hedge fund's legions of quants also were mesmerized by the sinking numbers. It was like watching a train wreck in slow motion. Work had ground to a halt that morning as everyone tried to assess the situation. Many of the fund's employees walked about the office in a confused daze, turning to one another in hope of answers. "You know what's going on?" The answer was always the same: "No. You?" Rumors of corporate collapses were making the rounds. Banks and hedge funds were reeling from their exposure to toxic subprime mortgages. Countrywide Financial, some said, was imploding and looking in desperation for a white knight, such as Warren Buffett's Berkshire Hathaway or Bank of America. But no one wanted anything to do with the distressed mortgage lender. Inside his office, [one hedge fund boss] again stared grimly at his computer screen. Red numbers washed across it. He didn't know what to do. His greatest fear was that there was nothing he could do.[5]

This was a financial disaster that many of us remember too well—and many are still recovering from. One can hardly imagine how surprised I was, in this context, to see that Mandelbrot's name had come up once more. He had seen it coming. It was no surprise. He had published his findings. But no one listened. Like Cassandra, he had seen the future but no one believed him. He had seen what others did not see, could not see, did not want to see.

> In a September 2009 article titled "How Did Economists Get It So Wrong?" in the *New York Times Magazine*, Nobel Prize–winning economist Paul Krugman lambasted . . . economists' chronic inability to grasp the possibility of massive swings in prices and circumstances that Mandelbrot *had warned of decades earlier*. Krugman blamed "the profession's blindness to the very possibility of catastrophic failures in a market economy. . . . As I see it, the economics profession went astray because economists, as a group, mistook beauty, clad in impressive-looking mathematics, for truth."[6]
>
> Among his many interests, Mandelbrot had been looking at cotton prices over long periods of time and had discovered wild or erratic moves. "Market prices, Mandelbrot had found, were subject to sudden violent, wild leaps. . . . The upshot of Mandelbrot's research was that markets were far less well behaved than standard financial theory held."[7]

Another unexpected connection with Mandelbrot's work is the modern cell phone, mobile phone, or smartphone that so many of us carry in our pockets or bags. The phones receive and send voice and data over various radio frequencies—and each frequency would usually require different kinds and lengths of antennas. As radio astronomer Nathan Cohen noted in a NOVA documentary on fractals, you would need a kind of porcupine with many different antennas sticking out of your phone for it to work properly and well. But there is another way.

Cohen had heard Benoit Mandelbrot give a lecture on fractal patterns in astronomy—making reference to self-similar fractal shapes. This suggested to Cohen that if he bent a piece of wire into one of the fractal shapes, it might work well for many different radio frequencies. In 1988, Cohen tried it and to his surprise it worked perfectly—right away. Cohen did further investigations and found that the fractal shapes were not only one possible solution to the antenna problem—they were the only good solution.

Consequently, all of us are carrying around in our pockets phones that rely on small fractal antennas first suggested by Mandelbrot's work. As Mandelbrot says in the NOVA documentary, "Once you realize that a shrewd engineer would use fractals in many contexts, you would better understand why nature, which is shrewder, uses them in its ways."[8]

I believe that Mandelbrot's original perceptions and contributions to so many different fields are great examples of what can be done by a brilliant visual thinker or different thinker when freed from the bounds and limits of specialist training and practice. Of course, It was helpful that Mandelbrot had been originally hired by IBM because he was known to be a different thinker.

"BEING DYSLEXIC"–THE MIT DISEASE

The varied talent mix of dyslexics seems to be especially well recognized in the world of computers—where performance is measured by demonstrating working systems and where anticipating technological trends is more highly valued than paper credentials and traditional academic skills.

One of the leading visionary thinkers in the computer field is Nicholas Negroponte, the dyslexic founder of the Media Lab at the Massachusetts Institute of Technology (MIT). More than a decade ago, he and others started work to form the Media Lab, which was to be based on the idea that major industries—such as publishing, telecommunications, television, feature film, and computers—would all converge rapidly over time until at a certain point it would be hard to tell which was which. Of course, now these predictions are seen as splendidly and universally justified, as we are daily confronted by the reality of these expectations.

In early 1995, Negroponte published *Being Digital*, a book of essays—based on a series of columns in the magazine *Wired*—about the likely and varied longer-term effects of the computer revolution. Since the book is so explicitly focused on computers, it is quite remarkable that the first and last sentences of his introduction, "The Paradox of a Book," refer not to computers but instead to his own dyslexia and his difficulties with reading. The book begins: "Being Dyslexic, I don't like to read books." And pages later we read, "So why [have I written] an old-fashioned book . . . especially one without a single illustration?"[9] He gives several reasons. Among these are the advantages inherent in the vagueness of words. When you read, he notes, more is left to the imagination and more is drawn from your own personal experience. In contrast, he observes that "like a Hollywood film, multimedia narrative" provides such detailed and realistic representations of things that "less and less are left to the mind's eye." Consequently, finishing his introduction, he says: "You are expected to read yourself into this book. And I say that as someone who does not like to read." Thus, we see a remarkable example of one of the leading and most prescient communicators of the digital revolution referring in his book repeatedly to his own reading problems. It is also notable that on radio programs during his book tour for *Being Digital*, Negroponte observed that links between dyslexia and talent are often observed at MIT; indeed, these observations are so frequent that sometimes dyslexia is called "the MIT disease."[10]

Some months later, Negroponte was featured on the cover of *Wired* magazine to celebrate the Media Lab's first ten years. Playing on the title of Negroponte's book, the *Wired* article begins: "Being Nicholas—The Media Lab's visionary founder . . . is the most wired man we know (and that is saying something)." During the interview, Negroponte is asked whether he would rather read text on a computer screen or on paper. His answer reveals the matter-of-fact, by-the-way manner in which many successful dyslexics have come more and more to speak of their difficulties: "I don't read long articles period. I don't like to read. I am dyslexic and I find it hard. When people send me long [e-mail] messages, I ignore them. The only print medium I read every day is the front page of the *Wall Street Journal*, which I scan for news of the companies I am interested in. All the rest of my reading is on screens, and often not very good screens, because I travel so much."[11]

SEEING THE RHYTHM

Other examples of successful dyslexics are not hard to find in the computer industry, in all its varied forms. The story told to me by one young programmer/designer is especially helpful in indicating the complex interplay of unusual strengths and weaknesses in this expanding field. He explained that he had been diagnosed as dyslexic in high school but nonetheless had been able to make his way through college, studying computer science. For some years, he has been working for a major manufacturer of advanced computer graphic systems, where he has helped to design the graphics hardware. It is important to understand that in graphic systems, speed is extremely important.

In this context, this young man told the story of how, along with his dyslexia, he found that he has a special and unusual ability that his coworkers do not have. He explained that he could visualize the design of an entire graphics system in his mind's eye. He could run the system in his head and see the pulsing and the rhythm of the data moving through the various circuits. And, using his mental model, he found that he could see where the bugs and bottlenecks were. For example, he could say that if the loads of a certain set of chips were balanced differently, then the system would go 20 percent faster. His coworkers felt that it was impossible to know this kind of information without doing extensive simulations. Several weeks later, when the simulations were finished, it was found that the corrected designs got exactly the performance increase that he had predicted.[12]

In viewing this case, we need to consider that this particular computer graphics company may have a considerable national and international competitive advantage, partly because they are making use of the special talents of one key dyslexic worker—one who is using talents that no one yet really understands. Indeed, one could say that this company became a world leader in its industry in part because of an employee who still has a lot of trouble with reading, writing, and spelling.

DYING SPIDERS AND MENTAL MODELS

As with the programmer-designer above, the new mix of talents and skills needed in various parts of the computer industry seem to provide a natural opportunity for some dyslexics. The following long passage is part of an e-mail message I received from a programmer in Britain. It provides an artfully worded and elegant profile of a pattern of dyslexic problems and special strengths that could be much more common than we would expect. It also serves to show how classic dyslexic difficulties interact in one family situation. I am struck, once again, by the way these special capabilities, although little understood, seem to be so well suited to the changing requirements of this particular industry—and the way someone who has trouble with words can write so well.

About 2 months ago the BBC showed a program in the Q.E.D. [popular science] series about dyslexia and learning difficulties . . . in which you were featured. I had before heard of various famous people being linked to dyslexia, especially Einstein and Churchill. But until seeing your piece in the show, I think I generally assumed, like most people, that they were great men who had [just] overcome their difficulties to lead distinguished lives. I had not heard before the theory that their abilities could be a result or side effect of their dyslexia. I must say I find [this theory] most interesting. I do not work in any field of research associated with dyslexia but have suffered with the problem all my life.

As you can probably see, my spelling leaves a little to be desired and if you could see it you would know my handwriting is closer to spiders dying than text. However, I have never had any problem expressing myself verbally and have always been told I am very creative. I read very slowly and find new words difficult to read. . . . I avoid reading aloud as I tend to read very slowly and with little expression which generally gives the impression I am unintelligent. I can never be sure to get left and right correct [the] first time.

Unfortunately, my mother used to be an English teacher and so finds all that kind of thing second nature. For a long time, she did not really believe that dyslexia existed but put my problems down to the usual sort of things—laziness, doesn't concentrate, late developer, etc. My father has the same sort of problems as myself and it is a family joke that my mother used to send his (love) letters back to him with the spellings corrected! My education was mainly at boarding schools and my letters home got much the same treatment. The English teacher at school had the same attitude as my mother and the Headmaster was convinced that beating me enough would knock the laziness out of me. . . .

Anyway, that is just some background. Now back to the subject of your theory (and book). I have bought your book and am reading it (slowly !). I studied, and work in, computers and have done since I was 16. I have always found the subject extremely easy and can produce quite complex systems in very short time scales to a great degree of accuracy and reliability. This is based around an "intuition" I have for the way computers work. Once I know the different aspects of a system I can understand all the implications of a single change on the whole, in a way I find that my colleges cannot. They have to analyse each part of the system trying to work out the effect a change will have on that part before going on to the next part and analysing that, etc. This "higher" ability over my peers is something I have only realised more recently and your theory came at just the right time to help me explain the situations I was being faced with.[13]

It is especially significant that this programmer found that once he has internalized a mental model of the whole system, he can quickly see the effects of any change. This method of working is entirely different from the step-by-step analysis one sees generally in conventional usage and education. Yet this is the same method of working that one finds often in discussions of the ways that highly sophisticated and complex problems are approached by highly creative people. It may be possible that a methodical study of young dyslexics such as these, working in different parts of this new industry, may yield new understandings of problem-solving strategies that may have broad applicability.

When we survey a few recent examples of highly successful dyslexics and visual thinkers, we can see that they have many strengths that are often not properly recognized in school or university but come to recognized in work and in later life. What can be learned from this puzzling pattern? It seems clear that we need to work on finding better ways of identifying and developing the gifts and talents that are often hidden under the difficulties of dyslexia and thinking differently. Also, when we look at highly successful individuals such as those above, we see that they succeeded by following their substantial gifts, not by focusing mainly on their difficulties. We need to find ways of bringing traditional education more in line with the requirements of work and life. The more we are able to do this, the more likely we will, in the long run, genuinely help dyslexics and visual thinkers—as well as the larger society. We are also likely to learn more about the true nature of talent and intelligence in the process.

SEEING THE PUZZLE WITH ONLY TWO PIECES—
LEARNING DIFFERENCES AT GCHQ

In June 2006, I was invited to travel to the United Kingdom to be the main speaker at the Diversity Day conference for the code-making and code-breaking descendants of Bletchley Park (World War II code breakers). It was the first ever Diversity Day for the employees of GCHQ (Government Communications Headquarters) in Cheltenham, England. Among the many brilliant linguists, mathematicians, engineers, analysts, scientists, and technologists employed at GCHQ, there are a number of individuals with dyslexia, ADHD, dyspraxia, Asperger's syndrome, and other learning differences—indicating that it is not unusual to find some form of learning difficulty or learning difference coexisting with certain very high-level talents and capabilities.[14]

The Diversity Day was a fairly high-profile event and program. They had even printed note pads. At the top of the note pad was a view of a brain with the words "Different Thinking." At the bottom was the GCHQ Diversity and Disabilities contact Web address. All of this used to be top secret. However, in more recent years, organizational pride in their diversity-support policies for "different thinkers"—and their desire to recruit these different thinkers—has resulted in talking publicly and listing their accomplishments and diversity policies on the GCHQ website. Indeed, a recent look at the website shows that diversity of all kinds is a major theme in their operations and hiring. Their phrase is, "Success depends on great minds not thinking alike."[15]

GCHQ now resides in a new, round building that everyone calls "the doughnut." Outside the doughnut is a smaller building that is the Visitor Centre, where the gathering took place. I will not give any details of my personal experience there, although it is not very different from other organizations to which I have been asked to visit and give talks. However, there are several public sources that help us to see what is possible when an organization seeks to recruit and employ individuals of highly varied talents—to do an important and most challenging job. The differences are acknowledged and relied upon. It seems that GCHQ can help us see what might be needed in all kinds of modern organizations in a time of rapid change, innovation, and new forms of threat.

As I quoted at the beginning of this book, GCHQ officials and cyber experts make it quite clear that their dyslexic employees, among others, are highly valued workers. As one spokesperson said in an article from the *Daily Mail*, "Dyslexia Is Britain's Secret Weapon in the Spy War: Top Codebreakers Can Crack Complex Problems Because They Suffer from the Condition": "Most people only get to see the jigsaw picture when it's nearly finished while the dyslexic cryptographists can see what the jigsaw looks like with just two pieces."[16]

Since "outsiders are granted access only sparingly," of special value is a carefully controlled public window into GCHQ, provided in a newspaper article called "Spy Brains," in the *Sunday Times Magazine*.[17] This source provides several examples of how various kinds of different thinkers, those who are not "neurotypicals," fit in and are highly respected at GCHQ. The 5,300 workers in GCHQ are described as "unseen heroes." Their identities are secret, and some experience conditions that range "from dyslexia to prosopagnosia" (having difficulty with recognizing faces). "Their unique brains make them brilliant at certain tasks," says the article—and "GCHQ needs brains that are wired differently."

One example cited in the article is the work of an analyst with dyspraxia named Harry. He was given a couple of days to solve a national security problem that some thought impossible to solve. Harry said he went into "tunnel vision" mode. He set out to solve the problem that his boss said was "not logically achievable." He worked with colored pens and a notepad and began doodling until he finally solved the problem. "I was given a needle in a field full of needles," he said. "I started trying stuff and then not following through, then trying something else and generally being completely upside down, back to front, and all over the place about how I did it."

Later, he succeeded, and his achievement earned Harry one of GCHQ's top awards. He could not say more about what he had done or how he had done it, because he was concerned about giving away operational or technical details. We may wonder about what the task or solution was. But this does not matter as much as the revelation that these different thinkers and can do remarkable things when given the right task with the right support and respect.

The head of the neurodiversity program at GCHQ, Jo (according to the article), was sitting in on the interview with Harry. At the time, she was responsible for the more than three hundred men and women within the agency—those with dyspraxia, dyslexia, autism, Asperger's syndrome, or other "profiles of difference." She is dyslexic and dyspraxic herself and "understands Harry and his colleagues better than anyone in the organization." A former school teacher, Jo developed the neurodiversity program for GCHQ when she joined the organization eighteen years previously. "I've always had a particular interest in how the brain works," she says. "I apply a practical approach—after discussion and sometimes a formal assessment, we work out how the individual can operate more effectively."

Another staff member, Al, was a classic dyslexic at school, with low grades and said to be lazy. But he did well at computer science and eventually became the head of IT at GCHQ. Another case is Amy, then recently diagnosed with dyspraxia. She came to understand why she was clumsy and why she hated sports. She was a wiz with languages but could easily confuse numbers and had trouble with mental calculations. When at Oxford University, she got a double first in languages, including Russian. "She says her dyspraxia helps her process text very quickly in different languages, which gives her the ability to produce intelligence reports at great speed. . . . Amy says that while people with neuro-diversity may be viewed as 'odd or weird' they are 'fully accepted' at GCHQ."

Chapter Eight

VISUAL FAMILIES AND NOBEL PRIZES

NOBEL PRIZES IN THE OLD TRADITION

"Ididn't expect [a Nobel Prize] at all," he said, "in part because of the nature of the work. There was less science [and more engineering] in it than the things customarily honored by the prizes."[1] This is the observation of Jack S. Kilby (of Texas Instruments) coinventor of the integrated circuit, on being notified of his award.

The Nobel Prize for Chemistry awarded at the same time to Alan J. Heeger (UC–Santa Barbara) and Hideki Shirakawa (University of Tsukuba) for their work on conductive polymers also reflected the recognition of broad effects rather than pure science. "We're very excited," said Daryle H. Busch of the American Chemical Society, "because this award is in the old tradition. That is, it was given for work that has a very substantial impact on society."[2]

The shift back to an earlier tradition by the Nobel Prize committee may have reflected a growing recognition in the larger world of the deep value of applied work of broad impact as opposed to the highly theoretical work of relatively low impact that has commanded such high prestige in recent decades. Thus, these changes might be read as the small beginnings of a larger and more gradual swing back toward a greater respect for the less theoretical and more practical—for the hand, for the eye, and for image building in the brain.

For some time the major contributions of visual thinkers have been eclipsed in many fields by theoretical approaches that do not lend themselves to pictures or images or imagined models or hands-on manipulation. For a long time, we have been told with confidence that visual approaches were old-fashioned and somehow primitive. Modern scientists and mathematicians, we have been told, did not need images. Pictures and diagrams were for nonprofessionals, laypersons, and children.

But we may now see that sometimes things could be going back the other way. With new visualization technologies—and a new sense of missed opportunities with the old, narrow, specialist methods—researchers in many fields are becoming aware that in order to do really creative work, they may need to go back to visual approaches once again. So, perhaps, we come back again to the place where the most advanced and creative work is done by visual thinkers using visual methods and new visual technologies. Once again, pictures are not only for children.

REASSESSING VISUAL ROOTS AT GREEN COLLEGE

Quiet indicators of these powerful changes are beginning, here and there, over recent years, to gain broader attention. In one instance, on a bleak and rainy Saturday, a small but historic conference took place in England at Green College, Oxford University. With observations that will gladden the hearts of many strong visual thinkers, the conference presentations focused on high-level achievements in the arts and the sciences within families over several generations. Titled "Genius in the Genes?" and sponsored by the Arts Dyslexia Trust, the conference included an associated exhibition of art and scientific work from eight families. All of these families showed evidence of high visual and spatial talents along with troubles with words. Several members of each family were also dyslexic.

In a view that is contrary to most of the generally held beliefs in educational testing and educational reform, the speakers indicated that a very high level of creative achievement in the sciences has often come from the neurological resources linked to success in the arts. The speakers also indicated that some of those who have excelled most in their scientific achievements are from families with varied visual and spatial talents—ones that often have had trouble with words (and where some members may be dyslexic). As we are becoming increasingly aware, there does seem to be a kind of trade-off—very early brain development (largely controlled by genetic factors), seems to gain unusual visual and spatial proficiencies at the cost of some lack of proficiency in some language system.

Consequently, there may be various family members who have special strengths in art, design, computer graphics, visual mathematics, mechanics, or engineering—yet may have unusual difficulties with reading, spelling, arithmetic, rote memorization, or foreign languages. It is all part of a familiar pattern—which is continually repeated with variations, generation after generation. The pattern seems to continue through families, parents to children, always different in details, but frequently similar in the overall pattern of high visual strengths with notable language difficulties in some form.

ONE FAMILY—FOUR NOBEL PRIZES

One of the speakers at the Green College conference was Patience Thomson, the former head of Fairley House School for dyslexics in London and later a publisher (Barrington Stoke) of "books for reluctant readers." She spoke of her family in which there are many visual-spatial occupations in the arts and the sciences and no less than four Nobel Prize winners. She explained that all of the prize-winning achievements had a

SEEING WHAT OTHERS CANNOT SEE

high visual component. Thus, in a most remarkable example of the larger pattern, in this extended family, the exceptional visual and spatial capabilities that had contributed to so much creativity and innovation seemed to have been balanced by problems in other specific areas.

On her side of the family, the Nobel laureates were her grandfather Sir William Bragg (1862–1942) and her father, Sir Lawrence Bragg (1890–1971). They received a joint prize for x-ray crystallography. On her husband's (David Thomson) side, the Nobel laureates were his grandfather Sir Joseph (J. J.) Thomson (1856–1940), for discovery of the electron, and his father, Sir George Thomson (1892–1925), for discovery of electron diffraction.

She spoke of her famous father and the other outstanding scientists in her family, her gifted children, and the way the power of visual-spatial thinking has colored their lives and has contributed to many of the considerable achievements of the family. Along with the scientists among the Braggs and the Thomsons, there have been several artists, architects, TV producers, computer experts, and one actor, along with a number of other occupations for which the role of visual-spatial proficiencies is not so obvious.

However, over five generations of this family, with many children and grandchildren, there have been a number who have been dyslexic or mildly dyslexic. At the time, she reported, there are many great grandchildren who are still "too young to tell." Along with the award medals and family photographs, the exhibition showed drawings and paintings by family members, including a self-portrait by Sir Lawrence Bragg. (An interesting detail: most self-portraits show the painter looking at himself—whereas Lawrence Bragg arranged his mirrors to show himself looking off to one side. Clearly, notable innovations at every turn, large or small.)

An indicator of the enduring importance of Lawrence Bragg's work is that when James Watson wrote *The Double Helix*—about his discovery of the structure of DNA with Francis Crick—he asked Bragg (their boss at the time) to write the foreword, partly to allay critics of the controversial book. The use of x-ray crystallography pioneered by the two Braggs was fundamental to understanding the structure of this molecule that carries all genetic information—and it has been an essential technique ever since.[3]

THE ART IN MEDICINE

Another speaker at the Oxford conference was Terence Ryan, MD. Dr. Ryan described the story of "Doctor X"—who turned out to be himself. He recounted his own life story as a man who was a leader in his field of medicine (dermatology) but had substantial difficulties with his early education and his medical education because of his dyslexia. For example, with exams, he would often recognize accurately symptoms and conditions but would sometimes come up with the wrong Latin name.

However, in his practice and clinical observations, he found that he could be a leader and innovator because he could recognize disease patterns that his medical colleagues could not easily see. He suspected that he had greater powers of visual observation than many of his associates. He also thought that his dyslexia helped him to be more flexible and innovative in his thinking, coming up with theoretical approaches quite different from others in his field.

As an example of the creative inverted thinking that dyslexics sometimes exhibit, he described one of his own theories, one that is still controversial. Generally, it is taught that skin grows as its lowest layers and older cells allow themselves to rise to the top layers, where they slough off at the surface. He explained that from his point of view, cells would be unlikely to allow themselves to automatically rise to the top layers—as they would thereby be moving away from their food supply in the bottom layers. Consequently, he uses the novel alternative explanation that the cells that rise to the top are in fact inadvertently pushed out of the way by other cells that are in fact making their own way down toward the nutrient supplies in the bottom layers (near the blood supply). In many ways the final result is the same, but the actual process is quite different. Consequently, his associates see him as one of the important "lateral" thinkers in the field.

In spite of his extensive educational difficulties, his medical career has been highly successful. Now retired, he has been Clinical Professor of Dermatology at Oxford University and Vice Warden of one of the Oxford Colleges. He has been president of many of the national and international professional societies in his field, as well as being active in establishing regional dermatology training centers in Africa and Central America. He is "not easily confined by definitions," which has helped him break new ground and produce nearly four hundred publications. As a hobby, Dr. Ryan does colorful flower paintings—often exploiting visual ambiguities in which it may not be clear whether a garden stair goes up or down or whether a flower is inside or outside a frame.

A VILLAGE OF MILLERS AND CLOCKMAKERS

The Green College exhibition also included information about a family from the village of Blockley, Gloucestershire, England. Blockley was the home of small industries and craft workers long before the Industrial Revolution. Most of the town lies along the spring-fed, "never failing" Blockley Brook, "once a very vigorous stream, which, for a thousand years or more, drove many mills."[4]

This family showed remarkable continuity over many generations of involvement with occupations that require a high degree of visual and spatial talent—construction and operation of these small leased mills in the village, over hundreds of years—as well as barrel making and clock-making. One clock made by a family member was in use in a church in a nearby village for over 260 years, from 1695 until 1962.

In 1658, one of the family members (William Warner) immigrated to America, and settled in what was to be the western Philadelphia area. There, his descendants continued for generations in occupations and businesses that required talent in mechanics, invention, engineering, art, and craft. For example, Joseph Warner was a silversmith in the middle of the 1700s.

It happens that this writer is a descendant of this family on his mother's side. Although at the Oxford conference I spoke mainly of the visual-thinking scientists who preceded the Braggs and Thomsons, the Green College exhibition did include oil paintings by my artist parents (Anne Warner West and Charles Massey West Jr.), and sculptures by their grandson Jonathan West. It may be no surprise that within this visually oriented extended family, there are several likely or diagnosed dyslexics, including myself.

SEEKING FAMILY PATTERNS

I have to admit that when I was originally urged to submit samples of family art for the Green College exhibition, I was interested—but also reticent. However, in time I thought it might be interesting to look at our immediate family and then go back several generations to see what I could find. I think many families with high visual talents (with or without dyslexia) wonder about this sort of thing.

As I noted previously, the neurologist Dr. Norman Geschwind said that the dyslexia trait would not be so common and would not persist generation after generation (in its varied forms) if it were not good for something. So, I wondered, did it persist in our own family? If so, what was it good for?

My parents met in art school. Some would expect (not entirely seriously) that this alone might be a strong predictor of some degree of dyslexia in their children and grandchildren (along with, perhaps, visual talents). I wondered what forms it might take in each generation. So, I thought I would provide a few examples in the exhibition to provoke discussion about the possibilities. Perhaps it will provoke discussion among other visual thinkers and their families as well. (In the process, I came to realize that my book, *In the Mind's Eye*, is in some ways an attempt to answer the question, "what is it good for?")

ALWAYS SEEKING THE LEADING EDGE

Viewing visual strengths and verbal difficulties over many generations (through many changes in technologies and economies) can be remarkably instructive. We may be led to ask whether it is true, as some believe, that many of the early dyslexics and strong visual thinkers with reading, writing, and language problems quit their schools and small towns as quickly as they could—heading for the sailing ships and the railroads, the telegraph lines and early aircraft, the oil fields and gold mines.

Did they mostly leave the small towns or the established cities like London, Boston, and Philadelphia—and seek their fortune (in disproportionate numbers) in places like Australia, New Zealand, Canada, Texas, Alaska, and California? Did all the Swedes who could not read (and so were not permitted to marry), really immigrate to America, as one Swedish researcher speculates? I have had long discussions about these possibilities with members of some of the old oil families in Houston, Texas. There seems to be a number of dyslexics in these families, generation after generation—and the pattern would seem to fit, one way or another.

We may ask: how have varied strong visual traits contributed over time to both school difficulties and to remarkable innovations and inventions, within an ever-shifting technological context? Why do these individuals seem to be so often out in front of everyone else—especially when they seem to be able to move ahead rapidly with the minimum of book learning and paper credentials (while using their special visual-spatial abilities, creative imagination, and hands-on skills), often taking great risks?

Why do so many of today's entrepreneurs and technologists seem to fit this pattern? Why do there seem to be so many of these individuals in places like Silicon Valley? Whatever the time or place, some individuals seem to find ways to get away from the traditional books, the solid credentials, and the old ways of thinking, by creating things that are entirely new. (I have seen a lot of this among those in the leading edge of the computer graphics industry—where it is mainly an oral culture—since most are working way out ahead of courses, manuals, and lectures.) It seems to be a pattern that would be entirely familiar to individuals and families in which strong visual thinking is common.

Perhaps it is worth looking at some of these families over time to see whether there is evidence of these enduring traits over many generations—visual thinkers doing the things they can do best in whatever technological context is made available to them by their time and place. Perhaps then we could begin to answer the question, "what is it good for?"[5]

"LEFT BEHIND AT THE BEGINNING OF THE RACE"—
ONE LIFE STORY

Seeking another answer to this question, in recent years I have been asked to write about the positive aspects of dyslexia and the way these positive traits have been reflected in my own life story.[6]

As with the Oxford University conference, it is sometimes useful to look at family patterns and the way mixed talents will become evident in different times and economic circumstances. I hope that some of these stories might indicate a way forward for some dyslexics and parents of dyslexics. In my simple-minded way, I often say that I think that in dyslexic families, "everyone gets a sprinkling." As Norman Geschwind observed, the non-dyslexic brothers and sisters may often have dyslexic-related strengths as well.

In my own life story, the beginning is quite familiar. The story of a little boy who could hardly read at all for the first three or four years of primary school—and struggled for many years to keep up. For a long time, his greatest ambition was to not be at the bottom of the class.

Gradually, however, as the curriculum changed from rote memorization to larger concepts and logical thinking, the little boy began to see that he could do easily things that his classmates had trouble with—and that he could quickly see things that they did not easily see.

Over time, this little boy became an author of books about dyslexia, visual talents, and emerging computer graphic technologies. His writing led to invitations to give many talks, including talks in nineteen foreign countries. His first book has been translated into three languages—Japanese, Chinese, and, most recently, Korean. To his surprise (and to the delight of his publisher), over time, his first book became a classic—an "evergreen," as they say in the trade, a book that never stops selling.

"I was happy as a child. . . . I have been happier every year since I became a man. But this interlude of school [made] a somber grey patch upon the chart of my journey. . . . All my contemporaries and even younger boys seemed in every way better adapted to the conditions of our little world. They were far better both at the games and the lessons. It is not pleasant to feel oneself so completely outclassed and left behind at the beginning of the race."[7]

These are not my words. However, these words perfectly reflect my own feelings through most of my own early education. They are the words of Winston Churchill, writing in 1930 of his own early life. At this point, Churchill was a well-known public figure—indeed, one who many thought was well past his prime—although his greatest test and his chief accomplishments were not to unfold until nine years later, with the beginning of World War II.

PARADOXES OF DYSLEXIA

The field of dyslexia is full of puzzles and paradoxes. One of the greatest of these is that sometimes—perhaps one can say many times—the student who appears most dumb in the early years of schooling can be among the most capable and successful later on in the world of work—especially when the work is creative and innovative—involving the ability to ponder, to think deeply, and to see patterns that others do not see. It seems that some high-level powers take time to develop—and are not yet apparent in youth.

As one highly successful dyslexic scientist pointed out, it is not hard for a dyslexic to think "out of the box," because, as he says, "they have never been in the box."[8] In contrast, those who always could do quickly exactly what the teacher wanted (getting top grades and top test scores) can find it very hard—if not impossible—to have a really new thought or to deal successfully with a really new problem or novel situation. They find it easy to retain old knowledge, but they may find it nearly impossible to create new knowledge.

THE DYSLEXIC ADVANTAGE

Over the years, I have come to understand that one of the most important jobs for dyslexics is to see what others do not see or cannot see—as well as to introduce novel ideas that help to avoid the problems of "group think"—diverse brains generating knowledge and perceptions that ordinary brains would never produce.

As we have said, in recent years, dyslexia is coming to be seen, remarkably, as a significant advantage in an increasing number of fields—often linked to success in design innovation, entrepreneurial business, and scientific discovery.

For example, as we have seen, one of the founders of the modern study of molecular biology was dyslexic and described how he used his powerful visual imagination to see new patterns and develop fundamental insights into the links between the genetic code and the immune system (twelve years ahead of all others in the field). Later, a different scientist proved experimentally that he was right and received a Nobel Prize for this work.

A world-famous professor of paleontology tries to teach his graduate students how to think like a dyslexic so that they can see patterns invisible to others, patterns long thought impossible. The rest is "just memorization," he says, without innovation or significant discovery.[9]

In recent years, researchers have been discovering patterns in neurological structures that help to explain why many dyslexics are so good with high-level thinking, even though they have so much trouble with low-level thinking in their early schooling.[10]

For example, dyslexics are often highly proficient in big-picture and forward-looking thinking—seeing how complex things interact with each other, how a story line will develop, seeing the full potential in a new technology before others, seeing major business opportunities. When everyone else is terrified of the coming changes, often dyslexics and others with learning differences are the ones who see patterns and possibilities that others do not see—and welcome the changes and innovations.

PERSONAL DISCOVERIES

In my own early schooling, mostly in a rural public school system, I had learned to read very poorly and very late and had great difficulties with most primary school subjects. This was a puzzle to my teachers and a worry to my otherwise supportive parents.

Even in the comparatively undemanding rural school system, I could barely keep up. I could learn almost nothing by rote. I could not memorize. I could not retain exact texts or numbers. I had to have time to ponder and think. I had to understand. I needed to know the story. I had to find a way to visualize the information. Then, I would never forget.

I knew nothing of my own dyslexia at the time. I was not diagnosed until decades later—at the age of forty-one. But I did know that there were many things that I could not do but that were quite easy for my classmates. However, gradually, in the last years before college, the increasingly high-level content began to change what was wanted and what I could produce. Gradually, everything was transformed. The higher-level curriculum began to play to my strengths rather than to my weaknesses.

It is interesting to see how shifting to higher levels can be a great help to certain individuals—even in areas of relative weakness—as mathematics had often been for me. It is worth giving a few details. Before, I had trouble with arithmetic and "math facts," but in time I came to love geometry, log tables, and the slide rule (obviously, long before laptops and smartphones). Eventually—to my great surprise—I got good grades in a two-semester course on the core concepts, philosophy, and history of higher mathematics that I was required to take in college.

The math course required us to make up our own "cheat sheets" with formulas and equations. The professor said he was not interested in whether we could memorize the formulas. He wanted to see evidence that we understood the basic ideas and what you can do with the various forms of higher mathematics. We learned about Boolean algebra, truth tables, deductive logic, various forms of geometry and graphing, and the fundamentals of calculus, trigonometry, probability, and statistics—along with information about the lives of the major mathematicians and their historical context.

I was amazed and delighted to learn certain fundamental concepts—such as "conic sections," the way circles, hyperbolas, and parabolas can be seen as just different cuts through the double cone shape. I was fascinated by the ubiquity of the "curve of error," the normal distribution of frequency found in all of nature. On one level, mathematics was an impossible chore in working memory. On another level, mathematics was a set of powerful concepts that were not only intellectually satisfying but also could be applied in many areas of work, such as the emerging computer technologies that have so dominated recent decades.

I have always kept the math textbook we used, and I never would have written the math chapter of my first book if it were not for this two-semester course. I noted, for example, the actions of my literary friends when reading the early drafts of my first book. They just skipped over my math chapter since they could not imagine understanding or being interested in such a topic. As intended, this math survey course proved to be of great value in my much-later work in several fields—especially early on, in those involving quality control and redesign specifications for early computer management information systems. (My own first regular job involved working with mainframes and punch cards. Others did the programming, but I understood the basics of what was going on and specified what the programmers needed to do.)

The course also permitted me to appreciate the significance of radical new mathematical developments such as the fractals and chaos theory of Benoit Mandelbrot (which subsequently proved valuable in my observations and writings about the early development of computer graphics and other areas—including, amazingly, the stock market crash of 2007–2008).

In both high school and college, I had a lot of trouble with foreign languages. But I loved linguistics and the history of language. I still had trouble with spelling and my slow, faltering reading—but I began to see that I seemed to have a special knack for following logical arguments in philosophy, complex story lines in literature, and higher-level conceptual thinking in science and technology.

Strangely, it was by my final year of high school, before college, when I felt that I was getting more out of the readings than many of my classmates. I can still recall, in some detail, almost all of the readings we did during that year.

I then went on to a small liberal arts college that proved to be the right place, on the whole, for the further growth of these newfound capabilities. Remarkably, my major studies were English literature and philosophy (so many books to be read and understood). Later, I did graduate work in international relations. I found that I could do high-level work, but I had to be careful because I could easily be overwhelmed by large volumes of reading and by large volumes of data and details to be recalled and named on demand. I had no trouble understanding the fundamentals in many different fields—or, indeed, the not-so-obvious linkages between different fields.[11]

SCHOOL WEAKNESSES, WORK STRENGTHS

After graduate school and military service, I was employed by several consulting and engineering companies. First I was hired as a trainer, but I soon moved on to a range of projects—in a can-do, product-oriented atmosphere that I loved. I was involved with projects on early computer information systems, studies of the effectiveness of certain medical services, developing national energy plans and international trade (participating in one trade mission to four Asian countries and then leading another mission to three countries—to Japan, Korea, the Philippines, and Indonesia; and then to Thailand, the Philippines, and Indonesia). Eventually, I was the number two manager for a large five-year renewable-energy development and training program for engineers in Egypt, funded by the US Agency for International Development.

Throughout these work experiences, I found ways to work around my weaknesses and ways to exploit my talents and strengths. (For example, I learned to never mention a number unless I had it printed, and rechecked, in front of me.) Usually working with engineers, economists, or computer programmers, I had little formal technical training in each area, but I found that I could easily understand the fundamental concepts and technical projects at an appropriate level, sometimes better than the specialists. Others could be relied on for the data and the details. I could write about the projects, integrate the various parts, explain them to clients, organize the presentations, write the proposals, plan the projects, and, eventually, manage them.

SEEKING FAMILY PATTERNS

I didn't really begin to understand the common difficulties and the common patterns of talent among dyslexics until my own two sons started having problems in their early years of primary school. The idea that they were going to go through what I had gone through was a great emotional shock for me. Suddenly, I realized that I had to understand this thing that had been running my life—and, in part, the life of my dyslexic artist father, as well as other family members.

So I had myself tested for dyslexia. I attended dyslexia conferences and started the research that eventually became the book *In The Mind's Eye*. I soon learned that almost all of the professionals in the field wanted mainly to fix reading problems. But they mostly ignored the special talents that many dyslexics have. Coming from a family of visual-thinking artists and engineers—many with dyslexia or related problems and talents—I realized that there was more to the story than just reading problems.

My research and first book focused on these talents as no other book had done before—the neurological foundations, the case studies and profiles of famous people, and the growing role of new computer graphic information visualization technologies. As I did my research in the late 1980s, I could see that the world of technology was changing in fundamental ways—almost all in favor of the dyslexics and their distinctive mix of talents—while, of course, most conventional educators and institutions were then—and still are—blind to these changes.

I was amazed to suddenly realize that, in most cases, the major technological changes unfolding in recent periods required skills and talents that seem to come easily to many dyslexics (information visualization, big-picture thinking, seeing what is coming over the horizon, seeing patterns that others do not see, etc.)—while the things dyslexics have had the most difficulty with (e.g., rote memorization, spelling, rapid reading, and mental calculation) were becoming less and less important in the workplace. Few education experts, even now, seem to comprehend the inevitable consequences of these major and unstoppable trends.

I suspect that my strong focus on the talents of dyslexics is the reason that my first book is still very much alive today—and still regarded as radical new thinking—more than twenty-five years since the first edition was published in 1991. Even the university research librarians liked it. It was selected out of some 6,500 books as one of the "best of the best" for the year by the Research Librarians of the American Library Association (one of only thirteen books in their broad psychology, psychiatry, and neuroscience category).

Over time, the book has come to be highly regarded in many quarters. To my great delight, the late Dr. Oliver Sacks (the famous author of *Awakenings* and *The Man Who Mistook His Wife for a Hat*) came to write in the foreword to the second edition: "*In the Mind's Eye* brings out the special problems of people with dyslexia, but also their strengths, which are so often overlooked. . . . It stands alongside Howard Gardner's *Frames of Mind* as a testament to the range of human talent and possibility."

VISUAL THINKERS, VISUAL TECHNOLOGIES

Over the years, as noted before, I have been invited to give talks and workshops for scientific, medical, art, design, computer, and business groups in the United States and overseas, including for groups in Australia, New Zealand, Canada, Dubai, Hong Kong, Taiwan, Singapore, and twelve European countries.

In addition, I was recruited to write a regular series of articles and columns on the broad effects of visualization technologies for an in-house quarterly publication of the international professional association for computer graphic artists and technologists (ACM-SIGGRAPH)—a truly international organization with many creative dyslexics (and conferences as large as sixty thousand attendees, often in Los Angeles). Many of these columns have been collected into a book with the title, *Thinking like Einstein: Returning to Our Visual Roots with the Emerging Revolution in Computer Information Visualization.*

Attitudes toward the special talents of dyslexics have been changing, but very, very slowly. Gradually, non-dyslexics are beginning to see why it is important to have dyslexics involved in their innovative start-up businesses or their advanced scientific research projects. They realize that dyslexics and different thinkers can often provide fresh and unexpected insights that cannot be provided by even the smartest non-dyslexics.

However, no one could be more surprised that I am with the wide and continuing interest in my books and articles and the ideas they contain. As I started my book research long ago, it was more than a small comfort to me to know that Winston Churchill, for all his major achievements as a leader in time of crisis, had also—once—been at the bottom of the class, feeling "completely outclassed and left behind at the beginning of the race."

VISUAL TALENTS AND DYSLEXIA IN A WORLD OF ART— THE WEST FAMILY

In the foreword to the second edition of *In the Mind's Eye*, Dr. Oliver Sacks notes: "West himself is dyslexic—this, no doubt, has strongly influenced his life and research interests, but also gives him a uniquely sympathetic understanding from the inside as well as the outside."[12] Of course, Sacks is correct—my dyslexia has influenced a great deal. But there is more. My own special interest in visual thinking and visual technologies is doubtless also heavily influenced by the fact that my parents were professionally trained artists who met in art school.

It is noteworthy that both of my parents attained top student prizes at a time when classical representational art training was still important. Indeed, I now refer to my parents as among "the last of the American Impressionists." It was doubtless also important that my mother's side of the family included a long line of engineers, millwrights, artists, craftsmen, silversmiths, and the like—very visual, very hands-on.

It also might be significant that my mother, Anne Dickie Warner West, was mostly deaf from an early age—because she had had scarlet fever twice when very young (she was born in 1908, before antibiotics were available to treat such illnesses). She was taught to read lips. This fact probably encouraged her to use her high visual talents much more than might have been the case otherwise. It also taught my brother Charles, "Chip," and me, from our earliest days, to speak clearly and distinctly—and to make sure that we were understood, repeating back every message when necessary. It also taught us how much guesswork she had to do—which she did very, very well. I came to believe that lipreading gave her only half the message, or less. The rest had to be supplied by context and by high intelligence.

It is also relevant that my mother grew up in the small, slowly industrializing city of Wilmington, Delaware, a world that had then become a center for art and magazine illustration. In the late 1800s and early 1900s, magazine illustration was a highly profitable business. The successful magazine illustrator Howard Pyle started a school in Wilmington that trained famous representational artists like Violet Oakley and N. C. Wyeth (the father and grandfather of the even more famous Andrew Wyeth and James Wyeth). Since it was a small city, the families knew each other well. The Warner and Wyeth families even had the same pediatrician, Dr. Margaret Handy—whose portrait was painted several times by Andrew Wyeth.[13]

In this context, it is useful to take a look at some of the significant events in this family of artists. This establishes the foundation of the visual world in which I grew up. I first drafted the story that follows to be part of a future book on Charles Massey West Jr. and Anne Warner West, their lives and their art. However, I see that it fits well here to establish a greater appreciation for my personal life story and familial background. I had always known of my parents' major awards and prizes; but the story behind the story was not known to me until we recently discovered a show catalogue among old family papers. Much was revealed in the 1942 art show catalogue.[14] It has provided some of the background and context that eventually influenced my own view of the world.

The Narrows, 1942–Recognition for a Dyslexic Artist

In the autumn of 1942, *The Narrows*, a painting by Charles Massey West Jr., was one of the prizewinners at the Fifty-Third Annual Exhibition of American Paintings and Sculpture at the Art Institute of Chicago.

For West in 1942, it was not the top prize; but there he was, shoulder to shoulder with the top artists of the era—artists like Grant Wood, Edward Hopper, and Georgia O'Keeffe—who have come to represent, over time, the very best of a distinctly American form of art.

It is true that the year before, in 1941, the *The Narrows* had already been shown at the Corcoran Gallery in Washington, DC, and it had been published in *Art Magazine*. But this was somehow different. It wasn't the top prize. But it was major recognition in a major show among major artists of the time.

The Death of Grant Wood, Famous for American Gothic

In the fall of 1942, the Chicago show and its exhibition catalogue mainly honored Grant Wood, who had died earlier that same year. Wood had already become an icon of American painting. With images such as

American Gothic (of course, very well known), *Daughters of Revolution*, and *Good Influence* (all reproduced in the catalogue), Wood had linked humor and satire with pride in the simplicity of Middle America. Sometimes he used a flat, almost plastic palate, with smooth forms, high contrast, and deep shadows—a style that was not commonly seen again until the creation of Pixar computer animation films many years later.

Nighthawks–Edward Hopper's Triumph

The top prize that year at the Art Institute of Chicago had gone to Edward Hopper for *Nighthawks*, a canvas that was to become itself another major icon of American painting. Lonely people in a bright diner in a dark cityscape—which is now familiar in numerous magazine articles, satirical imitations, and young persons' wall posters—culminating as the central focus of the major show on Hopper in the East Wing of the National Gallery in Washington, DC, that closed January 21, 2008.

Art historian and commentator Robert Hughes called Hopper the most important painter of the period, and it is noteworthy that *Nighthawks* is the lone image that spans the backs of Hughes's multi-tape video history of American painting. It is also notable how pivotal *Nighthawks* was in Hopper's professional life. One writer noted in the National Gallery show catalogue: "In May 1945, having become famous and successful after his triumph with 'Nighthawks,' Edward Hopper was inducted into the National Institute of Arts and Letters."[15]

Hopper paintings have retained high interest and value even after many decades of fashionable nonrepresentational art. In one recent example, one of Hopper's paintings (*Blackwell's Island*, 1928) was sold at Christie's in New York, May 23, 2013. "Estimated at $15–20 million, it brought $17 million—making it the evening's top lot and setting a new Christie's record for a single work in an auction of American Art."[16]

Very Best of Distinctly American Painters

For West, it was not the top prize, but there he was, as we have seen, shoulder to shoulder with the top artists of the time—a group of artists who have come to represent the very best of a distinctly American art form during an important period of American art history.

In the show catalogue, West's short biographical sketch was listed in facing pages with other short sketches of the top prizewinners. Hopper's bio noted that his "early work aroused so little interest that he gave up painting for several years."

In West's bio, his hometown is spelled incorrectly, but his study at the Pennsylvania Academy of the Fine Arts in Philadelphia (PAFA, the oldest and most prestigious art school in America), which he attended from 1931 until 1934, is noted along with his then current teaching position (at the John Herron School of Art in Indianapolis, Indiana) and his award in 1934 of the Cresson Memorial Traveling Scholarship (as top art student, for four months of study and painting in Europe).

In the show catalogue, there are black-and-white photographs of the winning paintings. Hopper's *Nighthawks* is in the middle of the booklet, Plate VII, "Awarded the Ada S. Garrett Prize." One page leaf away is *The Narrows*, by Charles M. West Jr., Plate IX, "Awarded the Honorable Mention for Landscape."

It is interesting to note that the Wood and Hopper paintings figure prominently in the way the Art Institute of Chicago presents itself to the public even today—in 2017—seventy-five years after this show and catalogue. Proudly proclaiming itself as the finest museum in America for 2013 ("Winner, Voted #1 Museum in the United States, *Travelers' Choice* 2013"), the front cover of the short guidebook to the museum has a photograph of *American Gothic*—while the long guidebook shows a blown up detail section from *Nighthawks*. The museum shop even sells an expensive leather tote bag with the full *Nighthawks* painting shown on both sides.

Those Who Showed in the Exhibition but Did Not Win Prizes

Also listed in the 1942 Chicago show catalogue were paintings by well-known and not-so-well-known artists of the period whose work was exhibited but did not win any prize. (The full catalogue listing is quoted below; comments from this writer are in brackets.)

Some of those listed were associated with the Pennsylvania Academy (now known as part of the Pennsylvania Academy School or Pennsylvania Impressionists, or American Impressionists) or with the Brandywine School of painters in Wilmington, Delaware (started by magazine and book illustrator Howard Pyle, mentioned above), including N. C. Wyeth, Andrew Wyeth, and James Wyeth.

> Henriette Wyeth, born Wilmington, Delaware, 1907; lives in San Patricio, New Mexico, 233 [given here is the reference number for the paintings exhibited in this show], Portrait of N. C. Wyeth. [Daughter of N. C. Wyeth, sister of Andrew Wyeth, aunt to James Wyeth.]
>
> Peter Hurd, born Roswell, New Mexico, 1904; lives in San Patricio, New Mexico, 133, Prairie Shower. [Husband of Henriette Wyeth; much later famously commissioned to do portrait of President Lyndon B. Johnson.]
>
> Francis Speight, born Windsor, North Carolina, 1896; lives in Roxborough, Pennsylvania, 217, Scene in West Manayunk. [West's teacher at the PAFA; both Speight and West were students of Daniel Garber among other famous PAFA teachers. Speight and his wife, Sarah, were longtime close friends of Charles and Anne West (Sarah was their classmate). Sarah Speight painted a portrait

of the young Charles West (at art school) that now hangs in the West Gallery in Centreville. The West Gallery also owns a painting of another Manayunk scene, *Cliff House*, by Francis Speight.[17]]

Walter Stuempfig, Jr., born Philadelphia, 1914; lives in Collegeville, Pennsylvania, 218, Family Reunion. [West's classmate at the PAFA.]

Donald M. Mattison, born Beloit, Wisconsin, 1905; lives in Indianapolis, 167, Good-by. [Mattison was West's boss at the time. As director of the John Herron Art Institute in Indianapolis, Indiana, Mattison had recruited West, then at the University of Iowa, as a young, star teacher. Indeed, as it become evident later, Mattison had been hired at this time to bring in new, high-quality talent, capable of producing students who would win major prizes in the United States and Europe. See article by R. B. Perry in *American Art Review*, April 2011.[18]]

Thomas [Hart] Benton, born Neosho, Missouri, 1889; lives in Kansas City, 59, Negro Soldier.

Georgia O'Keeffe, born Sun Prairie, Wisconsin, 1887; lives in New York, 180, Red Hills and Bones.

Boyhood in Centreville, the Once-Busy Wharf Area

It was not the top prize. But it was a long way to have traveled for the boy from Centreville—a small river town on the Eastern Shore of Maryland that had been in many ways unchanged for more than a century. The town of two thousand people on the Corsica River in a timeless rural area of farmers, watermen, and shopkeepers on the Delmarva Peninsula had long been a virtual island between the Chesapeake Bay and the Atlantic Ocean. It was reachable from Baltimore or Annapolis, on the Western Shore of the bay, only by slow ferry boat or ancient steamer. The two bridges across the bay were not built until the 1950s and the 1970s.

Born in 1907, the young Charlie West had spent his boyhood mostly in the town's nearby wharf area (not far from the family home on Chesterfield Avenue)—not unlike Mark Twain's Tom Sawyer and Huck Finn—following the river traffic; absorbing outrageous local superstitions from the cooks, deck hands, and travelers; seeing plays and melodramas at the James Adams Floating Theater when it was in town; and escaping his four older sisters and his no-nonsense, small-town businessman father (who ran a dry goods store opposite the county Courthouse).

At the Centreville Wharf, the Source of Stories for *Show Boat*

The James Adams Floating Theater was a theater built on a barge towed from river town to river town around the Chesapeake Bay and other eastern seaboard locations, such as the Outer Banks of North Carolina. It was said (and we now know, correctly said) to have been the actual basis for the stories later used in the musical *Show Boat*.

The watercolor by Charles West, *The James Adams Floating Theater*, is signed "CW '36." Charles did several watercolors and oil paintings of this floating theater and related scenes. Stories from the lives of those living on this floating theater were, in fact, the actual basis for those later used in the novel *Show Boat* by Edna Ferber and the musical by Jerome Kern and Oscar Hammerstein II. The origins of the novel and the musical are recounted in a history of the James Adams Floating Theater—described at another location by historian Mark A. Moore (in Bath, North Carolina)—provided in the following passage:

> Edna [Ferber] finally beheld the arrival of the massive show boat. The *"James Adams Floating Palace Theatre came floating majestically down the Pamlico and tied up alongside the rickety dock."* The craft was enormous. Painted white with dark trim, the flat-bottomed vessel was 132 feet long, 34 feet wide, and drew 14 inches of water. The long rect-

angular barge—a full two stories high—kindled in Edna Ferber all of the romance and river lore that her studies had yielded thus far: "*There began, for me, four of the most enchanting days I've ever known.*" . . . Miss Ferber scratched furiously on a pad of yellow notepaper as [owner-actor] Charles Hunter, smoking steadily, spun his tale for Edna. "*It was a stream of pure gold,*" she confessed. "*Incidents, characters, absurdities, drama, tragedies, river lore, theatrical wisdom poured forth in that quiet flexible voice. He looked, really, more like a small-town college professor . . . than like a show-boat actor.*" . . . Miss Ferber initially resented the idea of a musical adaptation of her novel. But she signed a contract in November 1926, and was quickly won over by Jerome Kern's beautiful score, with lyrics by Oscar Hammerstein. One of the compositions written for *Show Boat* has become an icon of Broadway and cinematic song. . . . "*I must . . . confess,*" admitted Edna, "*to being one of those whose eyes grow dreamy and whose mouth is wreathed in wistful smiles whenever the orchestra . . . plays* Ol' Man River. . . . *I never have tired of it. . . . And I consider Oscar Hammerstein's lyric to* Ol' Man River *to be powerful, native, tragic, and true.*" When Kern first played and sang the song for Edna, "*I give you my word,*" she confessed, "*my hair stood on end, the tears came to my eyes, I breathed like a heroine in a melodrama. This was great music. This was music that would outlast Jerome Kern's day and mine.*" And so it has.[19]

A Balance Point

The prize for *The Narrows* wasn't the top prize. But in the fall of 1942, at the age of thirty-five, the recognition received at the Chicago show was special indeed—a kind of watershed, a balance point in his life as a painter and an artist, one generation removed from a family of farmers and shopkeepers.

It was only eleven years before that that West had won a full scholarship to attend art school at the Pennsylvania Academy of Fine Arts in

Philadelphia—mainly based at the Academy's Country School at Chester Springs, Pennsylvania.

It was only eight years before that that he had been awarded the top art school prize to study and paint in Europe—and had almost lost his life from appendicitis as the grand ship steamed toward France.

At the hospital in Paris, after his operation, he was befriended by a Hungarian countess and her rich American husband—and was invited to recuperate at their grand chateau near Paris. In so doing, he saw, first-hand, the last days of a style of life—with lush gardens, expensive cars, grand estates, and grander parties—that was to end forever only five years later—when war broke out in Europe in 1939.

Influence of French Impressionists

In his painting, West loved the dash and freshness and vitality of the French Impressionists of the 1870s, 1880s, and 1890s. He saw it as a style well suited to the rural landscapes and river scenes that he had known all of his life.

Two years before the Chicago show, in 1940, West had married a fellow art school student, Anne Dickie Warner. Their first son had been born in March 1941, and he was named after his father and grandfather—so the baby became the third Charles Massey West, known as "Chip." A second son was born in August 1943—named Thomas Gifford West (with a middle name from his maternal great grandfather, Frank Gifford Tallman).

Upon seeing the Chicago catalogue, the man who later became the head of the Pennsylvania Academy sent a note to the former student:

> Dear Charlie: I can only take time for the merest word this morning, but the Chicago Art Institute catalogue has just come to my desk and I see that you have crashed through again. Heartiest congratulations and best wishes for all the Wests! Sincerely Yours, Joseph T. Fraser, November 11, 1942.

When the Chicago show closed December 10, 1942, America had been at war for its first full year. The art school closed. West was retrained to become a draftsman in the local war industries in Indianapolis, as an employee of the P. R. Mallory Company.

Thirty years later, after resettling his young family in his own hometown and having taught painting, sculpture, and history of art at several schools, art schools, and colleges—eventually—at the end of December 1972, at the age of sixty-five, West's life came to an end.

He was buried, with a small family service, alongside his parents in the family plot in Centreville (eventually, under one of the plain classical tombstones that he himself had designed), as flights of geese flew overhead in the cold of early January.

The West Gallery on Lawyers Row

West's wife, Anne, turned a small building, former law offices on Lawyers Row in the center of the town, into a gallery to honor both her husband's paintings and those of others.

West's father's dream was that his son would become a lawyer, the top of the social scale in the small agricultural town and county, a northernmost outpost of very Southern rural attitudes and traditions. It is no small irony that West's paintings—his art and his career so much a puzzle to his father and virtually everyone else in this essentially provincial town and rural county—finally ended up at the center of the law offices that face the old Queen Anne's County Courthouse. There, property deeds had been exchanged and fought over for hundreds of years—land ownership long having been in the area the main path to wealth and social position. Over the years, Anne West painted a number of views of the courthouse from the rented building, former law offices, which eventually became the West Gallery.

Anne Dickie Warner West—descended from an old Quaker family of millwrights, silversmiths, artists, and engineers (as well as sailing ship captains and, later, one famous movie stunt pilot—Frank Gifford Tallman—the third of that name) from Wilmington, Delaware, and, previously, Philadelphia (years before the arrival of William Penn)—lived on for another thirty-four years of painting and travel, grandchildren and family visits in Centreville and Chestertown—passing away in her sleep in the afternoon of November 10, 2006, at the age of ninety-seven, just a month short of her ninety-eighth birthday.[20]

Chapter Nine

CONCLUSION

Darwin ought to have been devastated by this assassi-
nation. The review was a distillation of the worst abuse
he'd been imagining for twenty years. In the months
leading up to the publication of *Origin*, he'd been so sick
with anxiety that his family and friends wondered if he
would survive the ordeal. Now everything he'd dreaded
had come to pass. . . .

But to his surprise, Darwin was troubled by Owen's
bile for only one night. "I have quite got over it today."
Far from wringing his hands, he was filled with a kind of
invigorating holy rage. . . . Charles Darwin . . . was redis-
covering a toughness that his sickly and retiring persona
had forgotten. The keystone of this new defiance was his
faith in his friends. It was they . . . who helped him feel
"bold as a lion."[1]

In this book, we have looked at a number of extraordinary people, some
who have done much to shape our world and the ways that we think
about it. However, it is remarkable how, in almost every case, there has
been resistance to these ideas—sometimes rude and even violent resistance. We began our story with James Lovelock. It seems fitting that we
end our story with Charles Darwin. Both have advanced remarkably
"simple" ideas—but ideas that continue to reverberate in every direction.

Darwin helped us to see how nature works and how we are a part of it. Lovelock helped us to see how nature, unwittingly, keeps our planet habitable for all life, including our own. They both saw what others did not see—often, they saw what others were not willing to see.

I love the story of Darwin's reaction to the criticism he had been dreading for so long. Once the worst had come, he was more than ready to fight on. This is an example for us all. By now, Darwin's key concept of "natural selection" appears to have been accepted by scientists all over the globe. It works so well to explain what is going on in the natural world. It is true, small pockets of critics survive in certain areas—but this criticism is based more on religious views than any real scientific consideration.

The story of the early acceptance of Darwin's ideas is wonderfully described in Iain McCalman's *Darwin's Armada: Four Voyages and the Battle for the Theory of Evolution*. The book describes the voyages of Joseph Hooker, Thomas Huxley, and Alfred Wallace—all had completed voyages in important ways similar to Darwin's original voyage on the *Beagle* in the years 1831 to 1836. Initially, they had many disagreements. But finally, under Darwin's influence, they all eventually came together to battle for an idea.

McCalman's book, like so many good stories, begins with the end—Darwin's funeral. Darwin had wanted a simple country burial. But others wanted more. His funeral took place at Westminster Abbey on Wednesday, April 26, 1882. "Twenty years earlier, the English press had taunted him as 'The Devil's Disciple.' . . . Now the *Pall Mall Gazette* spoke for all in comparing him to Copernicus and calling him the greatest Englishman since Newton. The more than 2000 mourners at the Abbey made up a Who's Who of the Victorian establishment. So many had applied for admission cards that the undertakers were rattled."[2]

WHAT HAVE WE LEARNED—AND WHAT IS TO BE DONE?

What can we learn from this group of remarkable people and their enduring struggles? I have come to believe that we, in our own small way, should follow the lead of Lovelock and Darwin, of Dreyer and Mandelbrot.

We need to focus on trying to gain acceptance of a small but important idea: visual thinkers and those with differently wired brains can sometimes see what others cannot see.

We should acknowledge that these individuals often suffer abuse in their early days of education, but can sometimes go on to do truly remarkable things in later life and work. We should work, like Huxley and others, to gain credence for these ideas—that these people should be recognized and cherished. That early failure can be followed by later success, large or small. That education and testing conventions should be changed to recognize these differences as well as the possible early signs of future accomplishment and discovery.

In the world of dyslexia, progress has been made over the some 120 years since the condition was first recognized. In the world of Asperger's syndrome and autism, some progress has been made in the roughly seventy years since these conditions were first recognized. There is so much more that needs to be done for visual thinkers, with or without these conditions, who are routinely belittled and dismissed by the conventional measures that still endure in education and employment. The deck is so often stacked against them. Often they are ignored. More often they are labeled deficient. Increasingly, professionals, usually with the best intentions, try to fix the problems. But almost no one looks at the emerging talents and distinctive capabilities of those who think and see differently.

SEEING A DIFFERENT KIND OF SEEING—TWENTY YEARS AHEAD

Some twenty-five years have passed since *In the Mind's Eye* was first published in the spring of 1991. Shortly afterward, two reviewers asserted that the book was some twenty years "ahead of current educational thinking." As a first-time author, I was, of course, greatly pleased to read this. But I did not take it very seriously at the time. However, over the years since, I have come to wonder more and more why so many efforts in school reform have so often ended in failure and how the perspectives outlined by me and others have been so uniformly ignored by the professionals—although not ignored by creative, visual-thinking dyslexics and other different thinkers, along with their families and a handful of insightful teachers and educational institutions.

I am beginning to think that perhaps we might get some different results if we were to see education through truly different eyes. Perhaps this might help us to understand how we can find islands of hidden talent in many students, all kinds of different thinkers, creating motivation and a sense of hope that never existed before—and so find ways to do less damage during all those years of education.

It is perhaps worth looking at one of these reviewers with some care to see what might be helpful. The following remarks were made by the late professor T. R. Miles, PhD, who, among many other accomplishments, was founder of the Dyslexia Unit at the University of Wales, Bangor (now the Miles Dyslexia Centre at Bangor University), and was the founding editor of the peer-reviewed professional journal *Dyslexia*. Professor Miles wrote:

> I entirely agree with [Dr. Doris Kelly] when she says that *In the Mind's Eye* is "about 20 years ahead of current educational thinking." Many of us have spent long hours considering all the things that dyslexics are supposed to be weak at. What Tom West reminds us of is that we need

to also consider dyslexics' strengths. . . . At present, so he implies, education is in the hands of those who possess all the traditional skills; and since not surprisingly, they assume that others are like themselves, the needs of some very gifted thinkers whose brain organization is different are not adequately met. I very much hope that both teachers and educational planners will read this book and take its message seriously.[3]

DIFFICULTIES IN SEEING PAST THE DIFFICULTIES

Professor Miles touches on an aspect that is almost never addressed but may be a major point in our considerations—that is, that most of the people involved in the study and remediation of dyslexia are not dyslexic themselves and were, in many cases, excellent pupils in their own school days. Accordingly, it may be very difficult for them see the emerging great strengths and creative powers possessed by the students sitting before them, who seem such helpless fools in doing even the most elementary academic work. Over the years, I have become more and more impressed with the extreme difficulty some professionals have in separating the concept of intelligence from academic performance and testing. Dr. Orton did not have this problem. With his first dyslexic patient, Orton made a point of identifying high intelligence that did not correspond to conventional academic skills.

Since Orton's time, too many seem to be like one individual who was head of a school for dyslexics, as described in the book *Reversals* by Eileen Simpson. Dr. Starr, she says, was full of good intentions in helping the struggling children. But, apparently, Dr. Starr was completely unable to believe that the children in her school could be highly intelligent. She thought Simpson, who was working at the school, was bright and capable—indeed, sufficiently able to follow her as head of the school. In the view of Dr. Starr, Simpson was smart—consequently, Simpson could not possibly be dyslexic herself. It is simply unthinkable. ("'What non-sense! . . . dyslexic? Impossible' she said.")[4]

We all may wonder how many in the field of dyslexic remediation harbor, deep down, the same beliefs as Dr. Starr, in spite of the best intentions and all protestations to the contrary. We may also wonder how many children pick up on these beliefs, buying into a life of low expectation and unrealized potential.

I am not arguing, of course, that all dyslexics have great talents—nor that all non-dyslexics are blind to the talents of dyslexics. But I believe we do need to consider that the kinds of talents they do have, great or small, may be just the kinds of talents that are invisible to conventional teachers and conventional tests and conventional measures of academic ability. This is why I believe that developing a whole new family of educational tests and measurement instruments is so critical.

In the ways of the world, it is a simple truth that one cannot be considered to be really bright unless there exists some test on which one can get a top score. And, as we have been trying to show, there are many talents and abilities that are important in life and work that are never measured by conventional psychological and academic tests. This needs to change.

To do this properly, it seems that we may need to get highly successful dyslexics involved in the process of test generation and implementation—because many conventional educators and test designers, with conventional training and assumptions, may be quite unable to see what needs to be measured, how it can be measured, and why it is important to create new forms of measurement. Old habits of thought are hard to break. But perhaps, once again, we will need to rely on dyslexics themselves to "see what others do not see or cannot see."

Clearly, it is time to develop new ways of assessing the strengths and weaknesses of students as early as possible. Sometimes great abilities can be hidden beneath striking difficulties. Sometimes, we are beginning to realize, the kid who is having a lot of trouble with reading or spelling or arithmetic may turn out to do very well indeed with astrophysics or advanced mathematics or molecular biology or film animation or computer information visualization—areas in which visual thinking and image manipulation are more highly valued than rapid recall of memorized names or math facts or large quantities of data. As we have seen, one major figure in the field of computer graphics told me that she estimated that half the people in the CG field were probably dyslexic—and her own extremely talented team members, those capable of immensely difficult feature-film work, were all dyslexic—100 percent.

Sometimes, when the conceptual context and the technologies change in dramatic ways, the high talents that were once marginalized or considered of low value in an old era may suddenly move to center stage, providing the exact set of skills required to do the most demanding work in the new era.

Somehow, we need to be able to observe these changes with an open mind. We must be alert in order to see potential and opportunity instead of only failure and restriction. Sometimes, we might discover, the kids who are having the most trouble should not be held back. Rather, sometimes, they should be pushed a long way forward—if the right area of potential expertise can be identified by a perceptive teacher or some new and innovative screening device or testing method.

There are many examples to show that those who are most gifted in higher mathematics can have persistent problems with arithmetic—and some of the best writers can never learn to spell. Identifying the right field for each specific student is important. It would help to hold their attention. It would build motivation. But, more important, it would allow them to use talents rarely recognized. Perhaps it would allow them to learn in ways that are quite different from conventional schooling (and out of conventional educational sequence).

Such changed perspectives would allow dyslexics and other different thinkers to gain respect from others for being able to do things that are challenging for other students—or even challenging for their teachers. For some, the easy things in primary school are quite hard; but the hard things in graduate school and work and life are quite easy.

In many cases, of course, such a new approach could be seen as an administrative nightmare. How can the system cope with such extremes of diversity, with so many different measurement scales? Life is so much easier when there is one scale—conveniently indicating those who are the top in everything and those who are at the bottom of everything. With some new system, with so many scoring high on at least one of several subtests, how do you know which ones are really bright and which ones are really not so bright? However, it is clearly not beyond our capacity to make it work if we are convinced that it must be made to work—if we are convinced of the real value of diversity in brains and abilities.

In this new era of interactive computer graphics, simulators, and scientific information visualization, we have many new and sophisticated tools at hand. And the need is great. It is high time to give up the illusion of uniformity and begin to take advantage—for the sake of these individuals as well as the needs of society at large—of vast differences in abilities in many diverse fields. When we all are having to compete with many millions of others globally (in an increasingly uncertain and changing economy; with fast transportation and cheap light-speed, long-distance communication), it is suddenly essential that all of us quickly find whatever special talents we have, and develop these to a very high level—whether or not it is part of the traditional academic curriculum.

True, it is not yet perfectly clear how this can be done. But it is clear enough that it will need to be done—and in ways that are very different from traditional educational pathways. And most likely it will require extensive use of information visualization and related technologies.

Sometimes just listening to the improbable life stories of highly successful dyslexics is enough to give us a few really new ideas about how to move forward.

Of course, not all will be able to move ahead quickly; but even the most limited student may have islands of strength that no one knew existed—ones that can be identified and developed early if we design the right tools. We must make it our business to help each different thinker to find these islands. Sometimes, almost anything will do to start. But in the end, it is really important for students to be able to say, "I have a lot of trouble with this, but I am the best in my class (or my school) at doing that." Sometimes, a whole life hangs in the balance.

DIVERSITY IN TIME OF NEED

Throughout this book, we have been dealing with diversity and mixed talents in many different forms. However, there are some deep questions that seem to lie under all of our considerations. We want superiority. So why do we need diversity? Perhaps the simplest answer is that we need many *kinds* of superiority—and that we cannot have it all at once. It seems that we should encourage diversity not only to be civil, not only to be respectful, not only to be humane, not only to be just—but also because we have a particular stake in diversity that is rarely, if ever, fully articulated. We want there to be people who have abilities we do not yet know that we need, abilities that we have not ever tried to measure, because we do not know that we needed them—abilities that may be in no way associated with the conventional abilities and talents that we now measure by formal or informal means.

As we have seen, adapting to change has been a major feature in human survival, as with all of life. We have made the point that as technology and other factors in the environment change, they sometimes substantially redefine the kinds of talents and abilities (and passions) that are wanted. The theory of multiple intelligences is very important in this discussion. If there is only one kind of intelligence (as many have been taught to believe), then you have only more of it or less of it. But if there are in fact many forms of intelligence, then the whole discussion is transformed. Accordingly, in this context, the main idea is that changes in the environment often occur too quickly for either evolutionary or cultural adaptation to respond. We are capable of learning and adapting in many ways and at many levels, but it takes time.

What we want, therefore, is to find means to tolerate and cultivate the talents in a wide diversity of individuals—with supportive institutions and organizations, so that when we need a certain set of talents and abilities, it is already out there, ready to be brought into service—sometimes, perhaps often, at the last moment, when finally it is realized that the old leaders or the old ideas are no longer working. Time is short, and radical, perhaps even frightening, changes must be made, regardless of the risks.

In the first description of developmental reading disability in the medical literature, in 1896, it was noted that one student could not learn to read in spite of "laborious and persistent training."[5] However, his headmaster observed that this student "would be the smartest lad in the school if the instruction were entirely oral."

From the earliest days, the central puzzle of dyslexia and other different thinkers has always been the linkage of high ability in some areas with remarkable and unexpected disabilities in other areas. For many decades, we have recognized this pattern, but we have generally focused only on problems. With the best of intentions, we have learned much about how to deal with some of the problems, but we have done almost nothing to develop a deeper understanding of the varied and hard-to-measure talents that come hand-in-hand with these seeming limitations.

CONCLUSION

THE OTHER HALF OF THE JOB—
NEW TECHNOLOGIES AND OLD IDEAS

I believe that the time has come to be serious about trying to understand the talents of dyslexics and other different thinkers. I propose that it is time to build a bold and ambitious program that will focus primarily on talent. We need to build a program with its primary focus on understanding and developing strengths and talents.

As a dyslexic myself, I feel a growing sense of personal responsibility to dyslexics and other different thinkers as a group. I feel the need to substantially change the course of what we are trying to do. I hold that we need to seriously embrace a radical change now, or there will be no change at all—allowing generations of different thinkers to suffer needlessly and wasting talents that are greatly needed by the society and the economy—as we enter an age of great uncertainty on many fronts. We badly need the big-picture thinking and original insights that seem to be the signature contribution of these individuals.

In my talks and writings since *In the Mind's Eye* was first published in 1991, I have long advocated a focus on special talents. Through case studies, I have tried to understand how these special talents are linked to dyslexia (and, more recently, other different thinkers) and how we can help children and adults to lead better lives by learning from the lives of highly successful individuals.

In many cases, areas of weakness are better understood. But when we look at high success in entrepreneurial business, artistic creation, technological design, or scientific discovery, we need to focus on what it is that these different brains are doing much better than those around them. I do not think we know this yet. How do we identify it? How do we measure it? How do we develop it once identified?

We do not yet understand it—but I suspect it has something to do with having a global view, seeing the big picture, having strikingly unusual insights, being able to build complex mental models, being able to look over the horizon to see things that others do not see, and observing patterns in nature and markets that others do not see or cannot see. These are not easy things to measure or understand. But we have whole families of new tools and technologies to do the job. We just have to be convinced that it is an important job to do.

As Harvard neurologist Albert Galaburda pointed out years ago, the brain research done in the 1980s could have been done some forty or fifty years earlier if only it were thought important to look at the wiring and microscopic structure of the brain. Dr. Samuel Torrey Orton had lamented, in his day, the same lack of interest in the structure of the brain. Sometimes old insights and perceptions are much more important than new technologies and trendy ideas.

I think we need to start talent-focused programs. We must not be mainly school-centered, as we are now. It is time for all of us to rethink what we should be doing in schools and colleges to prepare students for today's global economy. Often our thinking is imprisoned by our deeply held but outdated assumptions about what is essential for success in education, work, and life.

Careful investigation of the life and work and accomplishments of highly successful different thinkers—where insight and creativity are usually more important than conventional academic skills—will show us how wrong we can be. Technological change is redefining the kinds of things that need to be learned—trends that are often completely ignored by conventional educational debate. Many different thinkers excel at high-market-value creative and entrepreneurial skills while they often fail in low-market-value school-based skills. We need a serious and systematic study of the highly varied but distinctive talents. Again, it is clear that we need whole new families of tests and measures based on new assumptions.

SMALL THINGS AND SMALL GROUPS DO MATTER

We will have to deeply reconsider what we think we know about intelligence, talent, ability, and creativity. We need to develop new assessment tools beyond conventional measures, using new technologies, new insights, and new perspectives to measure capabilities not possible to measure before. It is likely that we will come to measure things we thought unimportant previously.

We should also note relevant trends in other fields. For example, there is a growing awareness in business and economic development literature of the high value of the innovative and entrepreneurial skills that many dyslexics exhibit. We need to recruit creative workers who understand unconventional areas of technology and talent and use them in their own work every day. We need to design conference programs that will be of interest to those working in these fields, such as engineers, designers, filmmakers, architects, scientists, computer graphic artists, and specialists in scientific information visualization—those who process and communicate information visually and graphically (using the most advanced computer technologies) rather than traditionally with words and numbers.

We need to do outreach to occupational groups that include many dyslexics, and learn to fully appreciate the kinds of special talents that many dyslexics have that are especially useful within these groups. For instance, we could provide talks and workshops for these groups at their own professional conferences and meetings. (Mostly, they would have no reason to come to conventional dyslexia conferences—so we must find ways to go to them.) We could work with professional groups to attempt to identify areas of talent especially well suited to certain tasks within these occupations.

Accordingly, I believe we need to push forward in several directions. We need to establish special grants for highly gifted individuals who exhibit great talent but also have areas of weakness or disability that would normally result in their exclusion from conventional forms of higher education and grant support. We need to develop mentor programs targeted to dyslexics of several different subtypes.

We need a range of scholarships designed for talented dyslexics—not to compensate for low performance—but to take advantage of idiosyncratic high performance, that is, to bring out high levels of hidden talent. We need to find funding for a series of documentary films, dramas, and other visual media that will communicate these insights and ideas to a larger audience— always moving past the usual concerns with problems and remediation to reveal the reality of vast potential and high-level talents.

THINKING "OUT OF THE BOX"

We need to assess the institutional changes required so that dyslexics and different thinkers with markedly mixed talents can still work within established larger institutional structures. We need studies of how this works and does not work. For example, as we have seen before, we can look at the relationship that dyslexic paleontologist John R. (Jack) Horner has with the Museum of the Rockies in Bozeman, Montana. The museum staff modified their procedures to do things in unconventional ways in order to allow Jack and his students to do high-level work, making dramatic discoveries, while designing new and highly innovative museum displays to communicate with the public.

Because of his dyslexia, Horner had flunked out of the University of Montana seven times. But he came to be known as one of the two or three most important paleontologists in the world—known as an original and innovative interpreter of the fossil evidence. Horner says he tries to teach his grad students "to think like a dyslexic" because that is where the "good stuff"[6] comes from—learning to read the book of nature with fresh insight without being distracted by the theories of others. He says the rest is "just memorization."

One of Horner's dyslexic students, as we noted, made discoveries thought "impossible"—finding red blood cells and flexible blood vessels inside a 68-million-year-old fossil bone. Horner pointed out that this discovery was never made before, because "all the books in the world" would say that it could not be done. Recall, he noted that it is easy for dyslexics "to think outside the box" because "they have never been in the box."

Finally, we need to be convinced that it is indeed time for substantial change. It is hard to see that, in a remarkable number of cases, true innovation in using the most advanced information visualization technologies comes, in fact, from those who have struggled most with the oldest technologies: reading and writing. It is becoming increasingly clear that new tools and new ways of seeing and discovering will require new talents and, often, different kinds of brains.

We need to see the truth of Horner's observation that dyslexia is "certainly not something that needs to be fixed, or cured, or suppressed!" Indeed, we need to see that, as Jack says, "maybe it's time for a revolution"—or at least "it may be time to start something."[7]

SCHOOL FAILURE, WORK SUCCESS

The view from the world of work can sometimes be quite different from the view from within the world of education. For some time it has not been surprising to see references to successful dyslexics in the conventional business media—as well as technology, politics, and other fields. Indeed, some time ago, in a now classic article, *Fortune*, a major American business magazine targeted to corporate heads, did a long cover article on dyslexic chief executive officers (CEOs), which included Charles Schwab (discount brokerage), John Chambers (Cisco), Paul Orfalea (Kinko's founder), Richard Branson (Virgin Group), David Boies (trial lawyer), Gaston Caperton (former governor of West Virginia), William Dreyer (scientist), Craig McCaw (early cell phones), and others.[8]

In fact, later, an entire issue of *Fortune* dealt with dyslexia, and Richard Branson, yet again focusing on the high success of the innovative businessman, mentioned his dyslexia only briefly in passing. On the cover of this special issue of *Fortune*, we see a photo of a broadly grinning Richard Branson (seated on a wall at home on his personal island, Necker, in the British Virgin Islands) with the text: "The Man Who Has Everything. The Money. The Family. The Island. (Damn Him.)" And on the inside: "The outlines of the story are familiar: He was a middle class British kid with dyslexia who nearly flunked out of one school, was expelled from another and finally dropped out altogether at age 16 to start a youth-culture magazine called *Student* that he hoped one day would be Britain's *Rolling Stone.*"[9]

So, we might ask, why does the popular press, especially the business press in the United States and the United Kingdom, seem to be so fascinated by highly successful dyslexics? Indeed, why do they seem to be so far ahead of professional researchers in this field—as well as research institutions and funding agencies? Are they just going for a sensational story—or are they tapping into something that merits close attention? Do the writers and editors and readers simply not understand the deeper nature of dyslexia—or are they seeing something more clearly because of their work-oriented focus? Are they dealing with highly successful individuals who are wholly unlike most other dyslexics—or are they looking at a group that could teach us much about the potential of all dyslexics (when they build their lives around exploiting their talents rather than correcting their deficiencies)? Is their perspective naive or wrongheaded—or, rather, are they helping us to refocus on the larger realities of life and work?

Years ago, Dr. Norman Geschwind had proposed that dyslexics should be expected to show evidence of certain forms of talent, especially with respect to visual, spatial, mechanical, and mental model building. Geschwind argued that the dyslexic trait would not be so common unless it conferred advantages over long periods of time. Also, he suggested that the same mechanism that produced the varied difficulties could produce the advantages as well. Clearly, from the earliest days, there were strong arguments for considering talents along with disabilities. However, something was lost along the way—as most professionals focused on problems rather than potential.

IMPOSSIBLE FIGURES, POSSIBLE MEASURES

In recent years, most dyslexia research has been oriented toward pathology—investigating what is wrong and developing means of remediation. However, some researchers—as well as some observers in the popular and business media—have long observed that many dyslexics have high visual-spatial and other talents that are enormously important for various occupations. Some have noted that when one seeks the most proficient in certain occupational groups—whether architecture, medicine, art, design, entrepreneurial business, engineering, computer technology, mathematics, or science—one finds that dyslexics and different thinkers seem to be well represented. Recent replicated research findings involving "impossible figures" suggest that appropriate methods for assessing the distinctive talents among dyslexics are now beginning to be understood.

Several years ago, one group of researchers hoped to better understand aspects of the talents of dyslexics by comparing visual abilities among dyslexic and non-dyslexic schoolchildren. To their surprise and consternation, the first set of tests indicated the dyslexics were mostly slower and less accurate than the non-dyslexic students. There was one exception, however. In one part, the test of what is called "impossible figures" (line drawings of objects not possible to construct in 3-D space), the dyslexic children were faster but no less accurate.[10]

Some thought that this was an unimpressive finding. Others felt that this finding might be very important, indeed—that it may be all that is needed to make a break into a deeper understanding of the dyslexic kind of brain and its distinctive (and hard-to-measure) special capacities. This task, unlike others, seemed to tap into apparently distinctive dyslexic abilities—seeing things as wholes rather than as parts, and an ability to perform better on novel tasks.

Briefly, it appeared that the other more conventional visual-spatial tests included a number of merely mechanical "traps" that tended to slow the dyslexics and make their answers less accurate—such as filling in the wrong circle on the wrong line of the answer sheet. On the other hand, the "impossible figure" tasks seemed well suited to the distinctive abilities of the dyslexics—as well as being relatively free of mechanical "traps."

With this in mind, a second study was carried out—with substantially similar results, largely replicating the previous study. The results of the two studies were reported in *Brain and Language* in an article titled, "Dyslexia Linked to Talent: Global Visual-Spatial Ability." In the discussion, these authors observe:

> Given that individuals with dyslexia typically read slowly, ... the finding that individuals with dyslexia are faster than controls on any task is surprising. The compelling implication of this finding is that dyslexia should not be characterized only by deficit, but also by talent.

Global visual-spatial processing (what we refer to as "holistic inspection") may underlie important real-world activities such as mechanical skill, carpentry, invention, visual artistry, surgery, and interpreting x-rays or magnetic resonance images (MRI). Linking dyslexia to talent casts this condition in far more optimistic light than linking it to a deficit only.... The discovery of talent associated with dyslexia may eventually lead to more effective educational strategies and help guide individuals with dyslexia to professions in which they can excel.[11]

Perhaps we might conclude, in spite of initial appearances to the contrary, that the authors of this study are indeed way out in front by looking at the talents of dyslexics—not only out in front of most other researchers but even out in front of the popular and business press as well.

LEARNING REALITY FROM FANTASY

In a documentary about the making of the *Lord of the Rings* films, the actress Cate Blanchett talks about the character she plays—but in so doing she also makes reference to the central concern of our own age, a fitting question for us all to ponder:

> I play Galadriel, who is the lady of light. Because she is the queen of the elves and the elves are passing over Middle Earth and moving beyond Middle Earth to the Grey Havens, there is a sadness, a bitter sweetness, about what Galadriel and her kind are going through. And she is handing on the torch to men, to humankind. And I think in a lot of ways she is challenging the viewers to say: What are you going to do with the Earth? We have had this paradise. So now you men, you humankind, you have the responsibility for this Earth. I think it is a very profound message. What are you going to do with the Earth?[12]

ACKNOWLEDGMENTS

I want to say that I am enormously grateful to those who have helped to carry forward the long-term effort to recognize, understand, and appreciate the distinctive talents of dyslexics and other different thinkers. I want to give special thanks to Fernette and Brock Eide, who have done so much to lead the effort in recent years with their books, conferences, websites, and the nonprofit organization they founded, Dyslexic Advantage (of which I am a proud board member). I also want give special thanks to Angela Fawcett for all of the work she has done to move the agenda forward in different parts of the world with her former editorship of *Dyslexia* and current editorship of the *Asia Pacific Journal of Developmental Differences*. I am full of admiration for the leadership of Lee Siang, Deborah Hewes, and the staff of the Dyslexia Association of Singapore in recognizing and developing the distinctive talents and capabilities of dyslexic children and adults.

My special thanks go to the late Oliver Sacks (and Kate Edgar) for the kind words and foreword provided for the second edition of *In the Mind's Eye*. My special thanks also go to Temple Grandin, who through her talks, books, and life story has done so much to open a window into the world of Asperger's syndrome, autism, and those "on the spectrum." I am grateful for the friendship and wisdom of the late Harold Morowitz, founding director of the Krasnow Institute for Advanced Study, and author of many books, including coauthor, with Eric Smith, of *The Origin and Nature of Life on Earth*. And finally, I am most grateful to my wife, Margaret, and sons, Benjamin and Jonathan, for their support and for teaching me so much over the years.

ACKNOWLEDGMENTS

Seeing What Others Cannot See is strongly linked to my previous two books and the people from whom I have learned so much for over twenty-five years. Many are thanked in my first two books, but most have provided influence that has extended to the present work. Those who have been especially helpful and supportive in the past and in more recent years, through conversations and meetings, and through their writings, publications, and films, are listed here: Will Baker, Donna Cox, Jim Blinn, Gordon Cameron, Janet Dreyer, John Everatt, Naomi Folb, Jack Horner, Harvey Hubble, Ken Hunter, Brandon King, Diana Hanbury King, Don and Mary Lindberg, Rod Nicolson, Adrian Noe, Sue Parkinson, Gavin Reid, John Elder Robison, Marc Rowe, Matthew Scurfield, Alvy Ray Smith, Delos Smith, Vijayasarathy Srinivasa, John Stein, Patience and David Thomson, and Jo and Richard Todd.

The quotations that introduce this book are from the following sources: Oliver Sacks, foreword to *In the Mind's Eye: Creative Visual Thinkers, Gifted Dyslexics, and the Rise of Visual Technologies*, 2nd ed., by Thomas G. West (Amherst, NY: Prometheus Books, 2009), p. 11; John Elder Robison, official website, 2017, johnrobison.com; GCHQ official, quoted in "Dyslexia Is Britain's Secret Weapon in the Spy War," by Robert Verkaik, *Daily Mail*, July 13, 2013; Beryl Benacerraf, quoted in "Beryl Benacerraf, M.D., Physician," by Alix Boyle, The Yale Center for Dyslexia & Creativity website, dyslexia.yale.edu/benacerraf.html; and Roger Parloff, "Deep Learning Revolution," *Fortune*, October 2016, pp. 96–106.

COPYRIGHT ACKNOWLEDGMENTS

The author is grateful to the following individuals, publishers, and companies for permission to reprint excerpts from selected material as noted below.

Thomas G. West, "Amazing Shortcomings, Amazing Strengths: Beginning to Understand the Hidden Talents of Dyslexics," *Asia Pacific Journal of Developmental Differences*, vol. 1, no. 1 (January 2014), pp. 78–89. Angela Fawcett, editor. Copyright 2014, Dyslexia Association of Singapore.

Thomas G. West, "Foreword: Why Some of the Best Writers Are Dyslexic," *Forgotten Letters* (London, England: RASP, 2012). Naomi Folb, editor. Copyright 2012, RASP, London, England, pp. 3–5.

The author has adapted sections from several of his columns and articles that appeared originally in the series Images and Reversals in various issues of *ACM SIGGRAPH Computer Graphics*, 1997–2001, Gordon Cameron, editor. The source of each excerpt, along with others, is provided in the endnotes for each chapter. This ACM publication makes no claim to copyright: "As a contributing author, you retain copyright to your article and ACM will make every effort to refer requests for commercial use directly to you." Subsequently, many of these columns and articles appeared in *Thinking like Einstein* (Amherst, NY: Prometheus Books, 2004).

LETTER FROM DELOS SMITH

Below is a letter I requested from Delos Smith. I initially wrote about Delos in *In the Mind's Eye*. Then we met at a conference and we became close friends. Delos had to have special language training when young. But for many years he worked for the Conference Board in New York City and became a favored radio and TV commentator on business issues. Long ago, I had read in an article on Leonardo da Vinci that he wrote in what is called "mirror writing" to keep people from understanding what he was writing. I did not know much at the time, but I strongly suspected that the expert who made this assertion was entirely wrong. Much later, I discovered that there are a significant number of people who quite naturally prefer to write in mirror writing. Indeed, they prefer to do many things in a way that would appear backward to most of us—including playing music and even speaking. Delos is one of these people. At my request, he provided some details about his life-changing experience associated with mirrored music. This is his story, so I decided to include it here without modification or commentary. I hope that his story will help to provide a better understanding of different kinds of brains and different kinds of minds.

—Thomas G. West

December 17, 2013

Dear Tom:

This is the story of "mirror day" when I played the song "Oh, My Darling Clementine" backwards (retrograde) and had my first musical feeling in my life. I played the song at 9:30 pm on Thursday, December 9, 1976. At 9:31 pm on that day my life had been changed completely. I didn't know that I would be leading a completely different life at that moment.

All I knew then was that I needed to ask a lot of questions about my early childhood challenges. I had thought they had been taken care of with my work with Sam and June Orton and Katrina de Hirsch. After their work, the Ortons declared that I was a "normal" boy and now could compete with my classmates. The date was September 1944. I was 9 years old and entering the 4th grade. From kindergarten through the 3rd grade I had been carried by my school—the Horace Mann School that was operated by Teachers College of Columbia University. The school was actually located in the Teachers College building. From September 1944 to December 9, 1976, at 9:30 pm I and my parents considered me "normal."

"Normal" was defined as having the ability to be able to comprehend the material in my school. This was true. I was able to comprehend the material but at the same time I was very inconsistent in my schoolwork. For the most part I did understand the work but at the same time I was puzzled by how my teachers were teaching me.

Then came December 9, 1976, at 9:30 pm when everything changed. At that moment I knew I had no understanding what my childhood problems were—and I had little understanding of what my work with the Ortons was all about.

I knew that starting in the 3rd grade I was pulled out of my classroom and directed to another classroom where I met with an Orton teacher who drilled me for an hour on the basic tools of the English language. These hourly classes started in the summer after I completed the 2nd grade. The special sessions would continue six days a week until I entered the 4th grade when I was then 9 years old.

When I was 34 or 35 years old, I decided to make a New Year's resolution. I had two traumas that I did not understand or comprehend. One was public speaking. Any public speaking terrified me because I would always speak some gibberish during my presentations. In schools my classmates found my mumbled language hilarious. As an adult it was just downright awful.

The other trauma was my total lack of musical ability—similar to other members of my family. I couldn't sing on key with others. In dance I was totally out of step. At college I was required to take ROTC for the first two years. My marching was a total disaster. I was never in step. In fact, I was almost thrown out of the college because I was out of step at an Armed Forces Day. I took dance lessons with Arthur Murray during college. After a few lessons the Arthur Murray people gave me my money back because they were unable to teach me. I also noticed that my parents had no musical ability at all and most members of my family had no musical ability at all either. The whole family was out of step. Why?

But I was a very good athlete. I shined in football, basketball and baseball. I was especially good in baseball. I was able to throw a baseball at a very high speed and was able to control the ball. This act required excellent coordination and rhythm but I couldn't dance or march.

One of my best friends had a beautiful singing voice and had been taking vocal lessons for years. I had gotten to know his voice teacher. In January 1970, I told this friend, Leo, my story and asked if he would he give me voice lessons. Leo said he would be delighted. I picked out some of my favorite songs and we started my lessons. After two weeks, Leo told me that he wanted to stop. He could not help me and he was taking my money without helping me at all. But if I insisted he said he would continue giving me lessons because he liked me so much. However, he felt I was hopeless. Some people just can't sing. We continued.

I took 3 voice lessons a week with Leo for several years. I had no sense of pitch and I had no sense of the rhythm of the song that I was attempting to sing. While I was taking lessons with Leo I decided to rent a piano. It took me a little while before I rented the piano because I was so intimidated that I couldn't enter the store. I felt the store people would yell at me that they only rented a piano to people that could play the instrument. Finally after a few attempts I entered the store and told them that I wanted to rent a piano.

It turns out, of course, that the people in the store didn't give a damn about my ability to play the piano but if I could pay the rental fees for the instrument. So I had myself a piano. Down the street from where I worked, a music school was now accepting reservations for the new semester. The Turtle Bay School of Music happily took my money. I did tell them that I was awful. They told me that this was no problem at all because they had teachers that could teach anyone if the student was willing to practice. I had heard this spiel from my dance teachers and my dance teachers had given up on me very quickly. I was still taking voice lessons and now I was taking piano lessons.

From my start in January, 1970, to December 9, 1976, at 9:30 pm, my progress in the performing part of music (singing and playing the piano) would have to be measured in millimeters, not in inches or yards. I, of course, went to a school where there were no grades at all. All you needed to do was to sign up at registration and pay the bill. But if I had taken the courses for credit I would have flunked all the performing parts. In 1973, I did take harmony and counterpoint courses. I now wrote lines of music. To the amazement of my teachers I was superb in writing music even though I couldn't play what I wrote. My teachers played my music and would just look at me and wonder how I could write such good music without being able to play the music. I didn't understand either.

In these seven years I attended nearly all of my classes. I rarely missed any. There was always homework that I did faithfully. I spent thousands of dollars on my music lessons and by most definitions I had only made marginal progress. Even though I could write music very well, I still couldn't play what I had written. At the same time even though I realized my lack of progress, I never wanted to stop in any way. I was always one of the first students to sign up for my musical lessons. There were, however, a few teachers who were not sympathetic to my cause—so I fired them immediately.

This is one of the pleasures of being an adult. I expected my teachers to be sympathetic to my cause and work with me. If they didn't, they were gone. I knew I was making progress. I felt that I was solving some type of mystery even though I had no idea what the mystery was. At no time did I think that my musical challenges had anything to do with my childhood challenges. I saw no correlation at all with speech and the written language challenges and my musical challenges. I didn't know how I was going to solve the challenges—but I was not expecting any major breakthrough.

On December 9, 1976, my class was orchestration. It was taught by my favorite teacher, Lucas Mason. Lucas made his living tuning pianos. He was, also, a composer and his instrument was the flute. For several years I only took classes with Lucas in the summer session. He would not allow me to take the winter or spring session because he felt that he could not help me and there were other students that were more worthy than I was. He was always amazed when I would show up for a summer session. This changed when he discovered that I could write music that I could not play. He played my music and just looked at me in disbelief. Now I was allowed to sign up for any course that he was teaching. I also took private lessons with him.

On that fateful day Lucas taught very popular compositional devices. One was called "retrograde." Retrograde was taking a theme of music and then playing the theme backwards. You could take that theme and play the theme upside down (inverse retrograde). Our example was Bach. He was a master of retrograde and inverse retrograde. Our job for those two hours (7:00 pm to 9:00 pm) was to hunt in what is called "the Bach inventions" for places where he used retrograde or inverse retrograde. I was able to find examples. Lucas, of course, found many more than I did.

I lived near the Turtle Bay Music School. When I arrived at my home from the school, I looked at my clock and it was exactly 9:30 pm. As my neighbor would start banging on the floor if I went later than 10:00 pm, this is why I knew it had to be 9:30 pm. On my way home I smiled to myself that I had started life by going backwards in my writing. I had never thought through about why I had mumbled language. Even though my mumbled language had cleared up for the most part, there were many times when I was intimidated or scared about having to speak publicly and I would return to my mumbled language once again. That evening, I had no thought that my earlier problems and my returning to mumbled language had anything to do my musical challenges.

I kept my songs on the top of my piano. I just reached up for any song. The song, of course, in this case was "Oh My Darling Clementine." I started playing the song from the end of the song to the beginning. I had played this song hundreds of times. I was pleased when someone could recognize it. I knew they thought it was worse version of the song that they ever heard. This never bothered me because they knew that I was playing "Clementine" even if it was terrible. But at that moment I had a surge of musical feeling that I had never experienced before in my life. I played "Clementine" backwards better than I ever played "Clementine" forwards.

For the next 30 minutes I played other songs backwards. I played Bach and Mozart backwards—until my neighbor started banging on the floor. I was absolutely stunned at this development. I had spent so much time trying to play music backwards (for me) and that turned out to be a very hard thing to do.

That night all I had then were questions. I knew I had a breakthrough, but I had no understanding of what it all meant. From December 9, 1976, to the present, I have been searching for an understanding of what all of this meant.

You have been a part of that exploration—and we will continue that exploration. See you on Monday.

Regards,

Delos Smith

DYSLEXIC ADVANTAGE–
DRS. BROCK AND FERNETTE EIDE

In March 2011, I received an advance uncorrected manuscript for a new book that was to be published that August. I was asked to provide a recommendation. This is what I wrote:

Here I provide my recommendation for *The Dyslexic Advantage: Unlocking the Hidden Potential of the Dyslexic Brain* by Brock L. Eide, MD, and Fernette F. Eide, MD, Hudson Street Press, publication date, August 18, 2011:

> "This book is destined to become a classic. After my many years studying the talents of dyslexics, I was pleased to gain from the Eides' systematic investigation a deeper understanding of how and why dyslexics often have a major advantage, working at high levels in many different fields—and why there is so much misunderstanding among conventional educators and employers.
>
> "Linking their broad clinical experience with the newest brain research, they illuminate many puzzles—such as why there are so many dyslexic entrepreneurs, why so many dyslexics choose to study engineering or philosophy, why dyslexics often see the big picture and see linkages that others do not see, why they often think in stories or analogies, and why some of the most successful authors are dyslexic.

"They explain why reading impairments should be seen as only a small part of a larger pattern—that dyslexia is not simply a reading problem, but a different form of brain organization, yielding remarkable strengths along with surprising difficulties.

"With new technologies and new business models, we can now see how the often remarkable talents of dyslexics will be in greater demand over time while their difficulties will be increasingly seen as comparatively unimportant. I am enormously grateful to the Eides for explaining why and how this is so.

—Thomas G. West, author of *In the Mind's Eye* and *Thinking like Einstein*

These words still reflect my basic approach to this wonderful book, which I continue to reread. With this book, and their previous book, *The Mislabeled Child*, the Eides have provided an important public service along with the nonprofit they founded, their websites, their conferences, and their energetic advocacy. They are both physicians and have vast clinical experience. This experience is coupled with a willingness to listen at length to the stories of their patients and families.

By listening, rather than merely administering standardized tests, often they have uncovered extensive giftedness (sometimes in several generations)—where many practitioners would only see pathologies and abnormalities that require repair and remediation. Their approach to these matters is, of course, very close to my own high interest in the talents of dyslexics and their development.

(In full disclosure, I should say that I have been working closely with the Eides for several years—and I am currently a member of the board for the nonprofit organization they established, Dyslexic Advantage—with the blog at DyslexicAdvantage.org.)

Some examples of the many short talks by individuals with dyslexia from the three small Dyslexic Advantage conferences in 2013, 2014, and 2015 (available on YouTube: www.youtube.com/user/Dyslexic Advantage) include:

Donald P. Francis, MD—Epidemiologist who worked on the Ebola outbreak in Africa in the late 1970s; central figure in the 1993 HBO TV film *And the Band Played On* (based on the 1987 book of the same name by Randy Shiltz) about the early days of AIDS in San Francisco and the difficulties of trying to understand the disease in a hostile political environment; discusses personal and family history related to dyslexia and the study of medicine.

Marc I. Rowe, MD—Written off as poor student in high school and was signed for a welding course; unexpectedly admitted to university on an athletic scholarship; went on to medical school and eventually became recognized as one of the top pediatric surgeons in the world, earning the top award in the field, the Ladd Medal; in his training, the clinical work was "easy"; then his discovery of surgery in medical school was "like coming home." At the DA conference, Dr. Rowe expressed his delight at being surrounded by dyslexics who could "finish his sentences."

Brandon King—Dropped out of high school with low grades; worked as assistant to dyslexic molecular biologist grandfather William J. Dreyer; soon was doing post-doc-level data visualization and using database tools at a Caltech laboratory; wrote computer tutorial to teach a professor about new computer-based visualization material—allowing the professor to understand the high value of the work done by a young PhD student. Brandon's talk received a standing ovation from the Dyslexic Advantage conference attendees.

John R. (Jack) Horner—Flunked out of university seven times; became

one of the top three paleontologists in the world; discovered the first
dinosaur embryos, among many other firsts; technical advisor to
Steven Spielberg for four *Jurassic Park* films; tried to teach his graduate students "to think like a dyslexic" to be able to make unexpected
discoveries, rather than just memorize what they have read in books.

Mimi Koehl, PhD—MacArthur Genius Award biologist; interested
in physics of how organisms interact; known for her interdisciplinary research approaches; informally diagnosed as likely dyslexic by another dyslexic MacArthur Fellow, Jack Horner, and
later officially diagnosed.

Erin Egan—Many early problems of dyslexia but had the skills and persistence for Harvard Business School and top jobs in corporate world;
has to read out loud to herself and pace the floor; can easily "read a
room" for what is not said for negotiations; willing to ask for help;
willing to take risks; first time talked publicly about her dyslexia.

David McComas, PhD—From "slow" to the interstellar frontier;
MIT-trained physicist working on cosmic wind from the sun
making up the "heliosphere"; as poor student in high school,
considered jewelry making as his future career; initially hired by
NASA for "fine assembly" skills; works in a largely oral culture
with whiteboard and group discussion; reading and writing are
difficult and rare.

Other Dyslexic Advantage conference talks of special note on
YouTube (topic "dyslexia and talent") include: Matt Schneps, scientist;
Julie Logan, dyslexic entrepreneurs; Larry Banks, filmmaker; Fernette
Eide, neurologist; Brock Eide, changing the paradigm; Rod Nicolson,
positive dyslexia; Manuel Casanova, neuroscientist; Catherine Drennan,
MIT professor; Sally Taylor, musician; Tiffany Coletti Titolo, adver-
tising managing director; and Scott Sandell, venture capitalist.

SOURCES OF INFORMATION

Provided below is a sampling of names and web addresses for a range of organizations, websites, and blogs that relate to the topics dealt within *Seeing What Others Cannot See*. Most sites will lead to many other organizations and sources of information. With the advent of Google and *Wikipedia* together with other search engines and ready sources of information on the Internet, web searches have become extraordinarily easy and rapid. However, with this ease and speed, the enduring problem of determining the reliability of information sources has become greater than ever. The organizations listed below should serve as helpful and reliable points of departure.

ORGANIZATIONS, WEBSITES, AND BLOGS WITHIN THE UNITED STATES

ACM-SIGGRAPH
(Special Interest Group on Computer Graphics
of the Association for Computing Machinery)
www.siggraph.org

Dyslexic Advantage
(Resources and articles about dyslexia, dyslexic advantages, learning strategies, dysgraphia and dyscalculia.)
dyslexicadvantage.org

APPENDIX C

Temple Grandin
(Dr. Temple Grandin's official autism website.)
www.templegrandin.com

International Dyslexia Association
(Based in United States with many overseas branches. Founded in 1940s
as the Orton Dyslexia Society, one of the earliest dyslexia organizations in
the world employing multisensory methods for teaching reading.)
www.interdys.org

InventiveLabs
(Dyslexic entrepreneurs.)
www.inventivelabs.org

In the Mind's Eye, Dyslexic Renaissance (blog)
(Thomas G. West, author, *In the Mind's Eye* and *Thinking like Einstein*.)
www.inthemindseyedyslexicrenaissance.blogspot.com/

Seeing What Others Cannot See (blog)
(Thomas G. West, author, *Seeing What Others Cannot See*.)
www.seeingwhatotherscannotsee.blogspot.com

The Krasnow Institute for Advanced Study, George Mason University
(Interdisciplinary research, computers, brains, and complex adaptive
systems.)
http://krasnow.gmu.edu/

Learning Disability Association of America (LDA)
www.ldanatl.org, www.idaamerica.org

Learning Ally
(Support for dyslexia and learning disabilities.)
www.learningally.org

John Elder Robison
(Website of author, advocate, and Aspergian John Elder Robison.)
www.johnelderrobison.com

Elisheva Schwartz
(Dyslexia Quest Podcast, interviews.)
www.elishaschwartz.com

Yale Center for Dyslexia and Creativity
http://dyslexia.yale.edu

ORGANIZATION WEBSITES OUTSIDE THE UNITED STATES

The Adult Dyslexia Organization (UK)
www.adult-dyslexia.org/

Barrington Stoke Ltd
(Super readable books for children.)
www.barringtonstoke.co.uk

British Dyslexia Association
www.bdadyslexia.org.uk/

Bundesverband Legasthenie & Dyskalkulie e. V. (Germany)
(Dyslexia and dyscalculia.)
www.bvl-legasthenie.de

Center for Child Evaluation and Teaching (Kuwait)
www.ccetkuwait.org/

Dyslexia Association of Ireland
www.dyslexia.ie

Dyslexia Association of Singapore
www.das.org.sg/

Maharashtra Dyslexia Association (India)
www.mdamumbai.com

POSTSCRIPT

With this book, I had hoped to provide some informal and sometimes personal observations and stories that would help different thinkers as they travel along their distinctive paths. I look back with some satisfaction that I have been able to share some useful insights—based mostly on the people I have met and what I have learned from them over twenty-five years. Indeed, in ways it has been somewhat like an artist's retrospective, including stories and excerpts from several different experiences and publications, some that have appeared previously in different form elsewhere.

I have also hoped that this book might influence the direction of future research and practice. But after more than twenty-five years, I'm painfully aware of how slowly these things change. So many are still focused on fixing problems; so few are looking at distinctive talents and ways to develop them.

I did not at first anticipate that my concern at this time would be that there are so many stories that I did not get to tell. Over the years that I have been gathering information, especially in more recent years, I realize that I have so much more material than I could use here. I have tried to select the best, old and new, and the most useful in developing a new kind of understanding.

I plan to use my new blog to share some additional materials. When you have a chance, have a look at SeeingWhatOthersCannotSee .blogspot.com. In addition, I have deliberately included in my bibliography and notes many references that have only been briefly mentioned. They are all of interest, and, I believe, will be well worth your time.

DIFFERENT THINKERS IN A TIME OF CHANGE

I believe it is time now for real change on many fronts—and I believe that the different thinkers we have been talking about will have a special role. Clearly, there have been islands of positive change in many parts of the country and in many parts of the world. But this is not enough. There is now a greater urgency.

We've talked about the influence of computers and automation and how this has affected education and employment. At the beginning of this book I quoted part of an article from *Fortune* magazine about the newest developments in neural nets and deep learning by machines. I made reference to the history of these developments by citing Norbert Wiener's observations in the 1940s about the expected effects of computers on employment. Some argue that employment problems have to do with international trade and foreign global competition. However, those who are well-informed see clearly that we are at threshold of greater automation of all kinds—and that this, not trade, has been, and will be, the main driver. And, as I have argued, the kind of education that we have been focusing on for many decades does not answer this imminent situation.

Indeed, I have argued that the kinds of things that many dyslexics and other different thinkers are good at—are the kinds of things that will continue to be more highly valued in the new economy that is now unfolding. As I have pointed out, over time, the machines have largely replaced low-level labor and then low-level clerical skills. Just now the machines are becoming increasingly capable of high-level pattern-recognition skills. This will become a major force for the next few years and decades. Our educational systems need to adapt to these new realities.

It is indeed a strange idea, but it is one that needs to be addressed seriously: Many of those who seem to need the most help in the traditional educational system may turn out to be the ones who will help the most with our adjustment to new economic realities. These different thinkers are often the real discoverers, the real innovators, the real disruptors. Much is said about the value of diversity. But rarely discussed is the most fundamental kind of diversity: diversity in brains and ways of thinking.

It seems clear to me that the abilities that we see among many dyslexics and other different thinkers are just the kinds of capabilities that will be needed more and more in the near future—and will come to be widely recognized as highly valued capabilities: the ability to see the big picture and not to be confused by details; the ability to integrate information from many different sources to build a deeper understanding; the ability to see entrepreneurial business opportunities; the ability to avoid thinking as a specialist in one narrow area; the ability to visualize complex systems.

I am hopeful that now—in a time of mounting crisis on many fronts—there will be a greater awareness of what different thinkers can contribute to the solution of many problems. I am hoping for greater awareness of the high value of the people who can see what others cannot see.

NOTES

CHAPTER ONE: SEEING THE WHOLE

1. As Lovelock tells the story in the BBC documentary, in September 1965, Lovelock met with Carl Sagan and another astronomer, Lou Kaplan. They had sheets and sheets of computer paper showing a complete analysis of the Mars atmosphere.

> What this analysis showed was that Mars had almost nothing but carbon dioxide. Just bare traces of other gases were present. And I knew immediately that this meant that Mars was probably lifeless. And at that moment, suddenly, a thought came into my mind: But why is the Earth's atmosphere so amazingly different?

This brief version of the story is supported by a much more detailed version from a long interview with Lovelock provided in "An Oral History of British Science" (in Partnership with the British Library) in 2010.

2. On YouTube, the BBC documentary titled *Beautiful Minds: James Lovelock*. Total time, 58:40. Lovelock's nonspecialist perspectives on science, the NASA Mars story, and related stories begin at time mark 25:50. With Lovelock mostly speaking for himself, this documentary is rich with important details about his early life, his unusual education, and how his unusual ways of thinking and working have led to major inventions and discoveries. Repeatedly we are told about how his "out of the box" and top-down, big-picture thinking led to insights that other over-specialized scientists could not see or were unlikely to see. They are mostly trained and hired to focus on narrow problems—so they have a hard time seeing the really big picture that requires the integration of knowledge and understanding of many related disciplines.

3. Prof. Tim Lenton, School of Environmental Sciences, University of East Anglia, quoted in ibid.

4. Makri, review of *Climate Change* by McMichael, January 27, 2017, p. 355.

5. William Dreyer, interview by Shirley K. Cohen, Pasadena, CA, February 18–March 2, 1999, Oral History Project, California Institute of Technology Archives, retrieved March 22, 2017, from the World Wide Web: http://resolver.caltech.edu/CaltechOH:OHDreyerW. Dreyer's high interest in his own visual thinking is evident in his first introductory remarks at the beginning of the five days of interviews: "I was just at UCLA two days ago with people studying brain imaging. . . . They tended to want a uniform brain, with everyone having the same anatomy and thinking the same way. That isn't at all true; it's amazing how different people can be. And in particular the book that I loaned to you—*In the Mind's Eye* by Thomas G. West—is about the only one I've ever seen that deals with the subject of people who have extreme visual imagery in the way they think. I wanted to preface all of this [set of interviews] with this little story, because . . . it has a profound implication." The passage quoted in the running text above immediately follows Dreyer's introductory statement. (Also, it happens that the Jim Olds mentioned here is the father of another Jim Olds, who happens to be the former director of the Krasnow Institute for Advanced Study at George Mason University in Fairfax, Virginia. Roger Sperry, Dreyer's near lab neighbor, also mentioned in this quotation, was Caltech Hixon Professor of Psychobiology from 1954 until 1984. Sperry was awarded the Nobel Prize in Physiology or Medicine in 1981.)

6. Janet Roman Dreyer, molecular biologist, second wife and widow of William J. Dreyer. Based on interview with Thomas G. West, June 28, 2005.

7. Tauber and Podolsky, *Generation of Diversity*, 1997, p. 207. In the words of Tauber and Podolsky, "This experiment marked the point of no return for the domination of the antibody diversity question by nucleotide studies: it was Susumu Tonegawa's final proof of the Dreyer-Bennett V-C translocation hypothesis through the use of restriction enzymes."

8. Multiple conversations with William Dreyer, Janet Dreyer, and

Brandon King, 2001–2004. Additional clarifications and further details were provided by Brandon King via e-mail, March 23, 2009. This additional material, supporting the summary descriptions provided in the main text, is provided here in full, with some light editing of the informal e-mail text: "Hi Tom, Thank you for forwarding to this to me. I did get a chance to review part of it and wanted to mention a few clarifications. One minor one is that while I have done visualization software, it is less than 20 percent, maybe even 10 percent of the work that I do and have done. I am [mostly] doing advanced programming developing databases/GUIs/tools [for] solving leading edge problems ([in] all of which I use my visual thinking ability to design the architecture of the programs), but many programs do not involve advanced visualization techniques. Handling the massive amount of data and tracking information about the data (meta data), requires a lot of software infrastructure that does not yet exist. Building the visualization tools that I would like to see requires this software infrastructure to be built in order to be able to pull all the right pieces together. While advanced visualization is one of my goals, like my grandfather, I've discovered the need to develop new infrastructure (tools/software) before building more advanced visualization techniques. So to summarize: I'm working on leading edge stuff, much of which has been the nonvisual software infrastructure (which I build by visualizing the components in my head, trying it out and fixing what doesn't work, before I write the code—much like my grandfather), but instead of turning gears in my head to build a new physical machine, I am designing, building and tweaking software infrastructure in my head. Also, when it comes to the story of the PhD student, I feel it's important to correct this one. . . . What happened is that each PhD student needs to [have a] publication in a scientific journal in order to receive their PhD. When he submitted his paper to the journal for review it was rejected because the reviewers couldn't understand the significance of the software (visualization + infrastructure) and how it was leading to some pretty amazing conclusions. What I did next was [that] I wrote a GUI (Graphical User Interface) that combined the infrastructure and visualization—which previously required that: (1)

you know how to program in the Python programming language and (2) could understand and use the clustering and visualization tools [provided] within Python—into a simple tool. This tool allows the user to load the data, do the clustering of the data, and visualize and compare the data using the advanced visualization tools the PhD student had written (all from an easy-to-use interface with no programming experience needed). I then took the data from the PhD student's paper and wrote a tutorial showing how to use the GUI to load and analyze the data much like the PhD student had done. The paper was resubmitted for a second review—this time with my name on it as well—which mentioned the GUI and tutorial in the paper. Upon [the second] review, one of the reviewers . . . changed their mind and said yes. [The reviewer] mentioned . . . [that] using the GUI and the tutorial gave [them] a better understanding of what the PhD student had accomplished. [It] . . . was hard to understand the significance without being able to use the tools. Since I was able to bridge that gap for the reviewers, the paper was accepted and published. I got my first publication, and the PhD student (who did amazingly advanced work, by the way, which is why the reviewers had trouble with it) got the publication he needed in order to meet the publication requirement for getting his PhD. That's pretty much it for clarification. Thanks again, Tom, for sending this along." [This long endnote is provided here to illustrate the use of high levels of visualization in everyday use in data display, computer programming, and scientific discovery.]

9. Brandon King's two papers: "Mining Gene Expression Data by Interpreting Principal Components," by J. C. Roden, B. W. King, D. Trout, A. Mortazavi, B. J. Wold, and C. E. Hart, *BMC Bioinformatics* 7 (April 7, 2006): 194; and "A Mathematical and Computational Framework for Quantitative Comparison and Integration of Large-Scale Gene Expression Data," by C. C. Hart, L. Sharenbroich, B. J. Bornstein, D. Trout, B. King, E. Mjolsness, and B. J. Wold, *Nucleic Acids Research* 33, no. 8 (May 10, 2005): 2580–94.

10. Personal communication, William J. Dreyer, August 1995. Quotation given is a paraphrase of the initial contact.

11. "Visualization Research Agenda Meeting," held February 15–16,

2000 (See West, "Summary"). This meeting, organized by the National Library of Medicine was intended to develop a research agenda on the impact of visualization technologies and possible implications for visual thinkers and dyslexics. New computer graphic and information visualization technologies are seen as an emerging force in redefining the abilities required to do high-level work in many fields—and as a unifying force across the traditional boundaries between science, medicine, art, history, geography, and culture. Participants included Donald Lindberg, director of the National Library of Medicine; Alvy Ray Smith, co-founder of Pixar and then at Microsoft Research; Jock D. Mackinlay, Xerox PARC; Gordon Sherman, Harvard Medical School and later New Grange School; James Olds, Krasnow Institute for Advanced Study at George Mason University; William J. Dreyer, California Institute of Technology; and others from NIH institutes and commercial and academic institutions.

12. Personal communication, R. S., March 2000.

13. Parts of this section have been excerpted from West, *In the Mind's Eye*, 2nd ed., pp. 309–17.

14. Gleick, *Genius*, 1992, p. 321.

15. Freeman Dyson, quoted in ibid., p. 321.

16. Gleick, *Genius*, 1992, p. 244.

17. Ibid., pp. 387, 388.

18. Ibid., p. 398.

19. Ibid., p. 388.

20. Ibid.

21. Michael Riordan, quoted in ibid., pp. 388–89.

22. Gleick, *Genius*, 1992, p. 389.

23. Sidney Coleman, quoted in ibid., p. 389.

24. Quoted in West, *Mind's Eye*, 1991, 1997, 2009, p. 26.

25. Gleick, *Genius*, 1992, p. 244. [Italics added.]

26. Feynman, quoted in ibid., p. 244.

27. Ibid., p. 245.

28. Feynman, quoted in ibid., p. 245.

29. Parloff, "Deep-Learning Revolution: Why Decades-Old Discoveries

Are Suddenly Changing Your Life and Electrifying the Computing Industry, and Why They'll Soon Transform Corporate America," *Fortune*, October 2016, pp. 96–106.

30. Weiner, *Cybernetics*, 1948, 1961, 1996, pp. 27–28.

31. Ibid.

32. *Economist*, August 1995, p. 71.

33. Gardner, *Frames*, 1983, p. 176.

34. C. Kleymeyer, personal communication, 1985.

35. West, *Mind's Eye*, 1997, p. 232. Parts of this chapter have appeared in different form in *In the Mind's Eye* and other articles and talks by the author.

36. Ritchie-Calder, *Age of the Eye*, 1970; Satori, *Surface Dysgraphia*, 1987, pp. 1–10; West, *Mind's Eye*, 1997, pp. 145–47.

CHAPTER TWO: VISUAL PERSPECTIVES

1. Gardner, *Frames*, 1983.

2. Geschwind and Galaburda, *Lateralization*, 1987; Geschwind, "Orton Was Right," *Annuals*, 1982; Geschwind and Behan, "Left-Handedness," *National Academy*, 1982. Parts of this chapter appeared first by request in a special issue of ACM-SIGGRAPH *Computer Graphics* (1992); later translated into German for the *Proceedings* of the 1993 conference where I was invited to speak to the fifty Max Planck Institutes (published 1994).

3. West, *Mind's Eye*, 2009, pp. 29–40, 101–75.

4. West, *Mind's Eye*, 1997, 2009.

5. Tyndall, *Discoverer*, 1870, pp. 7–8.

6. Ibid.

7. West, *Mind's Eye*, 1991, 1997, 2009.

8. Ibid.

9. Feynman et al, *Lectures*, 1963.

10. Campbell and Garnett, *Maxwell*, 1882; Tolstoy, *Maxwell*, 1981; Everitt, "Maxwell," *Springs*, 1983; West, *Mind's Eye*, 1991, 1997.

11. Everitt, "Maxwell," *Springs*, 1983.

12. Holton, "Genius," *Scholar*, 1972, pp. 104–106.

13. Einstein, *Papers*, 1987, pp. xviii–xxi.

14. Hoffman, *Rebel*, 1972, p. 25.

15. Holton, "Genius," *Scholar*, 1972; West, *Mind's Eye*, 1991, 1997.

16. Holton, "Genius," *Scholar*, 1972, p. 102.

17. Hadamard, *Invention*, 1954, pp. 142–43.

18. French, "General Relativity," *Centenary*, 1979, p. 111. (Quoted from Constance Reid's biography of Hilbert, 1970.)

19. Pais, *Subtle*, 1982, p. 172.

20. Based on sections from *Thinking like Einstein* (2004) and *In the Mind's Eye* (2nd ed., 2009). See also Nainoa Thompson, "Voyage into the New Millennium," *Hana Hou!* magazine, February/March 2000, pp. 41ff; Harriet Witt-Miller, "The Soft, Warm, Wet Technology of Native Oceania," *Whole Earth Review*, Fall 1991, pp. 64–69; Dennis Kawaharada, "Wayfinding, or Non-Instrument Navigation," Polynesian Voyaging Society, May 2002, http://leahi.kcc.Hawaii.edu/org/pvs/; and Sam Low, *Hawaiki Rising: Hokule'a, Nainoa Thompson, and the Hawaiian Renaissance*, Island Heritage Publishing, 2013. The *Hokule'a* has been sailing around the world since May 2014—and in January 2017 it had traveled through the Panama Canal and was in the Pacific Ocean once again, on its way home. See the Polynesian Voyaging Society, www. hokulea.com, and related websites.

CHAPTER THREE: SEEING ALONG THE SPECTRUM

1. Personal communication, David Prescott, July 15, 1984.

2. Source: Nobelprize.org.

3. Tesla, *Inventions*, 1919, 1982, pp. 31–33.

4. Ibid.

5. Ibid.

6. KPMG Peat Marwick, *Competitive Benefits from 3D Computing*, 1989, pp. 10 and 12.

7. Ibid.

8. Steve Silberman, "The Geek Syndrome," *Wired*, December 1, 2001 (available online at https://www.wired.com/2001/12/aspergers/ [accessed March 10, 2017]).

9. Amy Harmon, "Answer, But No Cure for a Social Disorder That Isolates Many," *New York Times*, April 29, 2004.

10. Dan Geschwind, quoted in Silberman, "Geek Syndrome."

11. Geschwind and Galaburda, "Lateralization," in *Arch. Neuro.*, 1985, p. 652.

12. Dr. Albert Galaburda, quoted in West, *In the Mind's Eye*, 2009, p. 39.

13. See books listed under Grandin's name in the bibliography.

14. Grandin, *Autistic Brain*, 2013, pp. 117–18.

15. Ibid., p. 119.

16. Ibid., pp. 6–16.

17. Robison, *Switched On*, 2016, pp. xx–xxii.

18. Robison, *Raising Cubby*, 2013, pp. 111–18.

CHAPTER FOUR: THE POWER OF DESIGN

1. Parker, "Shape of Things," *New Yorker*, 2015, p. 120.

2. Hayley Tsukayama, "Record-Breaking iPhone Sales Drive Apple's Revenue to Quarterly Record," *Washington Post*, February 1, 2017, p. A22.

3. Quoted in the biography by Walter Isaacson, *Steve Jobs*, New York: Simon and Schuster, 2011.

4. Leander Kahney, *Jony Ive: The Genius behind Apple's Greatest Products*, 2013, pp. xi and 1–2.

5. Fernette Eide, "Dyslexia Wow—Diagnosing Dyslexia from Its Strengths," Dyslexic Advantage (website), April 3, 2015.

6. Ibid.

7. Ibid.

8. Carolyn Hubbard-Ford, conversations with the author, July 2010.

Used with permission, with additions and revisions by Carolyn Hubbard-Ford, February 27, 2017.

9. Parts of this discussion appeared in different form in West, "The Abilities of Those with Reading Disabilities: Focusing on the Talents of People with Dyslexia," in *Reading and Attention Disorders: Neurobiological Correlates*, D. D. Duane, ed., 1999, pp. 225 ff.

10. Ibid.

CHAPTER FIVE: THOSE WHO CAN SEE

1. Calder, *Timescale*, 1983, pp. 25–26. An early version of this section appeared previously in the epilogue of *In the Mind's Eye*, updated edition, 1997, pp. 261–62.

2. Larry Smarr, e-mail to the author, 1994.

3. James Gleick, *Chaos: Making a New Science* (New York Viking), 1987, p. 47. Parts of this section have appeared previously in different form in ACM-SIGGRAPH *Computer Graphics*, vol. 33, no. 1, February 1999, pp. 15–17.

4. C. W. F. Everitt, "Maxwell's Scientific Creativity," in *Springs of Scientific Creativity*, Rutherford Aris, et al., eds. Minneapolis: University of Minnesota Press, 1983, p. 74.

5. Kenneth R. Jolls and Daniel C. Coy, "Art of the Thermodynamics," in *IRIS Universe*, No. 12, 1990, p. 35.

6. J. C. Maxwell to Thomas Andrews, November 1874, quoted in Jolls and Coy, "Art," p. 35.

7. Jolls and Coy, "Art," 1990, pp. 31–35.

8. Ibid.

9. Everitt, "Creativity," 1983, p. 79.

10. Lewis Campbell and William Garnett, *The Life or James Clerk Maxwell*. London: MacMillan; New York: Johnson Reprint Corporation, 1882, 1969, pp. 105–106.

11. Everitt, "Creativity," 1983, p. 121.

12. Ibid., p. 120.

13. West, "Otherness" quotation, in Folb, *Forgotten Letters*, posted inside the front cover.

14. West, foreword, in Folb, *Forgotten Letters*, pp. 1–2.

CHAPTER SIX: INSIDERS, OUTSIDERS

1. Gould, *Piggies*, 1993, 1994, pp. 427–28. In a long parenthetical note immediately following these observations, Gould further points out that the use of images is partly a matter of occupational convention. Here his technology references are dated, but the message is clear: "Natural scientists, although not noted for insights about communication, have better intuitions on this subject. Most scientific papers are illustrated, and slide projectors are automatically provided for scientific talks around the world. By contrast, I have, three or four times, suffered the acute embarrassment of arriving before a large audience in the humanities or social sciences, slides in hand, to deliver a talk that would be utterly senseless without pictures: no slide projector, no screen, not even a way to darken the room. My fault: I had forgotten to request the projector because, in my own scientific culture, slides are as automatic as words. . . ." So Gould advises young scientists to remember to ask for a slide projector if they are ever asked to speak before a department in the humanities. He says, "Call this Gould's law and let it be my immortality—long after everyone has forgotten those upside-down flamingos and panda's thumbs." I thought it worth quoting Gould's comments because this has been my own experience on many occasions—not, fortunately, because I had forgotten to ask for a slide projector (or video setup). For a long time, with organizers who are neither scientists nor artists, these technologies were considered expensive and perhaps not altogether necessary difficulties. Of course, there is no fundamental reason why literature or law or philosophy or history should be so adverse to illustration. There is clearly much to be gained in all of these fields through the effective use of the image. With the wider acceptance of new multimedia equipment in recent years, these factors may be

beginning to change. We may see it as a sign of growing cultural maturation when even lecturers in the humanities begin to feel the need for some form of imagery to balance their traditionally word-bound presentations.

2. It appears that the favorable comparisons given in *In the Mind's Eye* have been moving some way toward balancing this tendency. It seems easier to talk of problems that are shared by people like Einstein and Churchill.

3. Dyslexia Association of Singapore, "Lee Kuan Yew," 2015, pp. 5–6.

4. Ferguson, *Engineering*, 1992. p. 53. It is also notable in this context that the father of Jony Ive, the master designer for Apple Inc., worked against this trend in British schools and pushed for more, not less, hands-on education. Jony Ive's father helped to devise "an integrated course that mixed academics with making things." He also helped to write the a required curriculum so that England and Wales "became the first countries in the world to make design technology education available for all children between the ages of five and sixteen." (Kahney, *Jony Ive*, 2013, p. 3.) Reforms of this kind could have major effects, providing a path forward for many dyslexics and visual thinkers—not only for "practical" skills but also for many very high-level skills as well. Maxwell, Lovelock, and Dreyer were all very hands-on. They made their own instruments and consequently had a deeper understanding of the processes and quantities they were investigating. Too many educators focus on academic skills alone. Sometimes the most powerful combinations involve hands-on capabilities along with conventional academics.

5. See Zimmerman and Cunningham, *Visualization . . . Mathematics*, 1991.

6. Steen, "Patterns," *Science*, 1988, p. 616.

7. Park, *Study*, 1993, p. 162.

8. Davis, Porta, and Uhl, *Welcome to* CALCULUS&*Mathematica*, 1994, p. 11.

9. Beryl Benacerraf, interview with Alix Boyle, "Beryl Benacerraf, M.D., Physician: World-Renowned Radiologist & Expert in Ultrasound of Pregnancy," Yale Center for Dyslexia and Creativity, http://dyslexia.yale.edu/benacerraf.html (accessed March 7, 2017). Benacerraf explained how her

strengths had roots in something many saw as a weakness. (Benjamin R. West contributed this section.)

10. Dr. Beryl Benacerraf's father was the late Baruj Benacerraf, MD. Dr. Baruj Benacerraf passed away August 2, 2011, in Boston, aged ninety. He was Fabyan Professor of Comparative Pathology, Emeritus, at Harvard Medical School and was past president of the Dana-Farber Cancer Institute, Boston. A Nobel laureate for discoveries in immunology (1980 Nobel Prize in Physiology or Medicine), Dr. Benacerraf was recognized as a distinguished dyslexic in 1988, receiving the Margaret Byrd Rawson Award from the National Institute of Dyslexia. Together with his lifelong difficulties with reading, writing, and spelling, he observed that he (along with other family members) had a special facility with visualizing patterns in space and time—an ability that he believed contributed greatly to his scientific research and discoveries. Dr. Baruj Benacerraf said, in a letter of August 5, 1994, to Thomas G. West about his book *In the Mind's Eye*: "I would like to thank you for the copy of your book . . . which I read with considerable interest. I wasn't aware, and I am enormously proud that I share my learning problems with such distinguished characters as Albert Einstein, Michael Faraday, James Clerk Maxwell, Sir Winston Churchill, Gen. George Patton and William Butler Yeats. I found your detailed analysis of the various deficiencies very informative and I think your book is a real contribution to the field."

11. Horner and Gorman, *Build a Dinosaur*, 2009, pp. 30 ff. Recommended on "60 Minutes Presents: B-Rex" (YouTube video, 14:10, posted by "CBS News," December 26, 2010, https://www.youtube.com/watch?v=yJOQiyLFMNY [accessed March 7, 2017]), which provides many images of the findings.

12. Robert Service, "Paleontology—Researchers Close in on Ancient Dinosaur Proteins: 'Milestone' Paper Opens Door to Molecular Approach," *Science* 355, no. 6324 (February 3, 2017): 441–42 .

CHAPTER SEVEN: SEEING AND TECHNOLOGY

1. Plato, "Phaedrus," *Collected Dialogues*, quoted in Norman, *Smart*, pp. 45–46.

2. Partly adapted from West, *In the Mind's Eye*, 2nd ed., 2009, pp. 286–89.

3. Gleick, *Chaos*, 1987, pp. 86–87.

4. Benoît Mandelbrot, quoted in "Drawing: The Ability to Think in Picture and Its Continued Influence," a segment of his Web of Stories video interview by Daniel Zajdenweber and Bernard Sapoval, recorded May 1998, 3:28, uploaded January 24, 2008, available at https://www.webofstories.com/playAll/benoit.mandelbrot (accessed March 13, 2017). Text: "The late French-American mathematician Benoît Mandelbrot (1924–2010) discovered his ability to think about mathematics in images while working with the French Resistance, and is famous for his work on fractal geometry, the mathematics of the shapes found in nature."

5. Patterson, *Quants*, 2010, p. 211.

6. Ibid., p. 291. (I have added italics in this passage for emphasis.)

7. Ibid., p. 296.

8. Biographical information obtained from Fractal Antenna Systems, Inc., biography of Nathan Cohan (available at http://www.fractenna.com/nca_cohen_bio.html [accessed March 7, 2017]); antenna information from Nathan Cohen (2002) "Fractal Antennas and Fractal Resonators," US Patent 6,452,553. This story is told by Nathan Cohen in the documentary *Fractals: Hunting the Hidden Dimension* (Lisa Mirowitz, senior producer and project director; Evan Hadingham, senior science editor; WGBH NOVA, 2008).

9. Negroponte, *Being*, 1995, pp. 3–8. There are other incidental references to his dyslexia in the book. For example, in the acknowledgements section, on page 236, Negroponte writes: "Word by word, idea by idea, [my editor Marty Asher] nursed my dyslexic style into something that was one step away from bullets."

10. Negroponte, appearance on the "Diane Rehm Show," WAMU-FM, Washington, DC, March 1995.

11. Negroponte, quoted in cover interview, *Wired*, November 1995, p. 204.

12. R. M., personal communication, August 1993. Used with permission. (See also note 13 below.)

13. J. S., personal communication, e-mail, September 7, 1995. Used with permission. [Spelling errors have been silently corrected. British spelling has been preserved.] Parts of this section (and the section referred to in note 12 above) first appeared in *In the Mind's Eye*, updated edition, 1997, pp. 269–71.

14. According to the UK Dyspraxia Foundation: "Dyspraxia, a form of developmental coordination disorder (DCD) is a common disorder affecting fine and/or gross motor coordination in children and adults. It may also affect speech. DCD is a lifelong condition, formally recognised by international organisations including the World Health Organisation. DCD is distinct from other motor disorders such as cerebral palsy and stroke, and occurs across the range of intellectual abilities. Individuals may vary in how their difficulties present: these may change over time depending on environmental demands and life experiences." (Dyspraxia Foundation, "What Is Dyspraxia?" http://dyspraxiafoundation.org.uk/about-dyspraxia/ [accessed March 7, 2017]; British spelling preserved). It is notable that there is no mention here of special talents. However, those with dyspraxia working at GCHQ are often extremely talented linguists, sometimes able to speak ten or fifteen languages—languages sometimes learned in very short periods of time.

15. GCHQ, "GCHQ Diversity and Inclusion Festival 2014— Programme of Events," Program of events for the Diversity and Inclusion Festival held at GCHQ Cheltenham from 19–23 May 2014, available at https://www.gchq.gov.uk/gchq-diversity-and-inclusion-festival-2014-programme-events (accessed March 7, 2017).

16. Statements from GCHQ official and cyber expert, *Daily Mail*, July 2013: "Many of Britain's top code-breakers and analysts are able to crack complex problems because they suffer from dyslexia, GCHQ has revealed. A spokesman for the Government's top-secret electronic eavesdropping station in Cheltenham said last night that some of their most talented code-breakers have

difficulty in learning to read or interpreting words. But this can actually help them crack codes, as they 'see' things those without the disorder do not. . . . A GCHQ spokesman said some of their most talented code-breakers were affected [by dyslexia]: 'They are very creative but may need support.' . . . MPs on the commons Intelligence and Security Committee praised steps taken by spy chiefs to harness the skills of dyslexic code-breakers. . . . Adrian Culley, a cyber expert and former Scotland Yard computer crime detective, said: 'Dyslexic people have the ability of seeing codes with patterns, repetitions and omissions. Dyslexia may in other circumstances be regarded as negative—but most people only get to see the full jigsaw picture when it's nearly finished while dyslexic cryptographists can see what the jigsaw puzzle looks like with just two pieces.'" Robert Verkaik, "Dyslexia Is Britain's Secret Weapon in the Spy War: Top Codebreakers Can Crack Complex Problems Because They Suffer from the Condition," *Daily Mail*, July 13, 2013, www.dailymail.co.uk/news/article-2362793/Dyslexia-Britains-secretweapon-spy-war-top-codebreakers-crack-complex-problems-suffercondition. html (accessed March 7, 2017).

17. Jon Jones, "Spy Brains," *Sunday Times Magazine*, June 26, 2015, pp. 32–35. The general theme of the advantages of dyslexia is set forth in several ways by Malcolm Gladwell in his book *David and Goliath*, 2013, pp. 110-111. For example, he writes about the dyslexic lawyer David Boies. Boies says his dyslexia forces him to "simplify issues to their basics." In contrast, the opposing lawyers read and know too much so they "get bogged down in excessive detail" and lose the case.

CHAPTER EIGHT: VISUAL FAMILIES AND NOBEL PRIZES

1. Quoted in Curt Suplee, "Six Awarded Nobel Prizes in Chemistry, Physics—'Information Age' Contributions Honored." *Washington Post*, October 11, 2000, p. A2. An early version of this section appeared in *Computer Graphics* 35, no. 1 (February 2001): 16–17.

2. Ibid.

3. See foreword by Sir Lawrence Bragg, in Watson, *Double Helix*, 1968, p. 2.

4. Cotswold Wardens, *Country Walks*, 1991, p. 1.

5. See G. M. Caroe, *William Henry Bragg, 1892–1942: Man and Scientist*, 1978.

6. The personal brief life story provided here was originally requested by the British Dyslexia Association (BDA) and was used in two of their publications in 2012. Later, this story was also used in two publications of the Dyslexia Association of Singapore (DAS). In November 2014, I was invited to give a series of five talks in Singapore as a kickoff for the DAS project Embrace Dyslexia. The project, designed to take advantage of the distinctive talents of dyslexic children and adults, has resulted in a number of publications and other media, including several talks (by myself and other speakers) currently available on YouTube. As part of the effort, a book was published in 2015 that contains over fifty short stories of successful dyslexics in Singapore. The introductory section of that book includes a version of this personal story along with a brief description of the mild dyslexia of Lee Kuan Yew himself. ("Left behind at the beginning of the Race: The Paradoxes of Dyslexia," by Thomas G. West, and "Lee Kuan Yew: Singapore's Founding Prime Minister, Visionary, Leader, Father and Builder of a Nation, 1923–2015," in *Embrace a Different Kind of Mind: Personal Stories of Dyslexia*, edited by Deborah Hewes (Dyslexia Association of Singapore, 2015).)

7. Churchill, *My Early Life*, 1930, pp. 38–39.

8. John R. (Jack) Horner, personal communication with author, 2007.

9. Ibid.

10. See Eide and Eide, *Dyslexic Advantage*, 2011.

11. It is significant that we can also see this tendency in the work of James Lovelock and others. How can we design an educational and testing system that recognizes these capabilities? Too often conventional testing focuses on a series of facts—but not on the connections between these facts—especially when they are facts from different fields of study.

12. Sacks, foreword, *Mind's Eye*, 2009, pp. 11–12.

13. Wyeth, *Autobiography*, 1995, p. 98. "From the Capes, 1974," portrait of Dr. Handy, tempera on panel (Gallet C., Ltd., Japan). Andrew Wyeth's comment: "Dr. Margaret Handy sometimes let her hair fall down, and, boy, that was when her part-Indian blood rushed into her amazing Indian eyes! And she was usually so tweedy, so demure. I adored the contrast."

14. Art Institute of Chicago, 1942. Catalogue of the *Fifty-Third Annual Exhibition of American Paintings and Sculpture at the Art Institute of Chicago.*

15. Barter, 2007, p. 211. From Barter, Judith A., 2007. "Travels and Travails: Hopper's Late Pictures" in *Edward Hopper*, Boston, MA: MFA Publications, pp. 211–25. The book was published in conjunction with the exhibition "Edward Hopper," organized by the Museum of Fine Arts, Boston, the National Gallery of Art, Washington, DC, and the Art Institute of Chicago. Other sections of this book were written by Carol Troyen, Janet L. Comey, Elliot Bostwick Davis and Ellen E. Roberts. *Nighthawks* is so well known that a recent review of satirical images revealed no less than ninety-eight images on Google.

16. *Architectural Digest*, September 2013, p. 66.

17. David Sellin, 1986. "Francis Speight," in *Francis Speight: A Retrospective, November 7–December 6, 1986.* Taggart, Jorgensen & Putman, 3241 P Street, NW, Washington, DC, 2007.

18. Perry, Rachel Berenson, 2011. "Indiana Realities: Regional Paintings 1930–1945." *American Art Review*, Volume XXIII, Number 2, March–April 2011, pp. 68–75.

19. More, Mark A., "Historic Bath: Edna Ferber and the James Adams Floating Theater," http://www.nchistoricsites.org/bath/edna-ferber.htm. On rechecking this website in the ever-changing Internet, I was delighted to see that Mark A. Moore had much expanded his earlier treatment of the Edna Ferber/showboat story—providing more historic details and many additional illustrations about the author, the novel, the New York Algonquin connections, the country people of the Chesapeake Bay and Outer Banks areas as well as the players and the real showboat itself. Highly recommended. Rechecked, January 2, 2017.

20. A series of photographs of paintings and other artwork by Anne Warner West and Charles Massey West Jr. is available online. Instructions: Go to Google, click on photographs, and request "Charles M. West, Jr." Then click on this image to bring up the full set of fifty-nine images—including informal gallery photographs of oil and watercolor paintings, bronze and welded steel sculptures, art book references and sketch books from the 1930s. Click on each image for descriptive text. The full title on Google is: "Art Works, Charles Massey West, Jr., and Anne Warner West." (Rights for all West artwork, photographs, and papers are held by Thomas G. West.)

CHAPTER NINE: CONCLUSION

1. McCalman, *Darwin's Armada*, 2009, p. 341.
2. Ibid., p. 1.
3. T. R. Miles in *Dyslexia Contact*, June 1993, pp. 14–15. The late Dr. Miles was Professor Emeritus and founder of the Dyslexia Unit at the University of North Wales, Bangor. Parts of this section have previously appeared in different form in the second edition of *In the Mind's Eye*, pp. 317–21.
4. Simpson, *Reversals*, 1979, pp. 59–60.
5. Morgan, "Case of Congenital Word-Blindness," *British Medical Journal* (1896): 1378.
6. Horner and Gorman, *How to Build a Dinosaur*, 2009.
7. Ibid.
8. Morris, "Dyslexic CEOs," *Fortune*, May 20, 2002.
9. Morris, "What a Life," *Fortune*, October 6, 2003.
10. Von Károlyi, 2001; von Károlyi and Winner, 2003; von Károlyi, Winner, Gray, and Sherman, 2003; Winner et al., 2000; Winner et al., 2001.
11. Von Károlyi, Winner, Gray, and Sherman, 2003.
12. Cate Blanchet, "The Making of the Lord of the Rings," Subsection on Elves, Science Fiction Network, on DVD, 45 seconds.

BIBLIOGRAPHY

Agassi, Joseph. *Faraday as a Natural Philosopher*. Chicago: University of Chicago Press, 1971.

Agence France Press. "Why Lee Kuan Yew Was Lost for Words," *South China Morning Post*, Hong Kong, January 18, 1996.

Allen, William. "Scientific Visualization: Where Science and Art Merge." In *Supercomputing Review* 2, no. 8 (August 1989): 28–30, 32–33.

Alsever, Jennifer. "Is This Robot a Friend—Or a Foe? Automated Manufacturing Technology Is Becoming Affordable for Smaller Companies. What Does That Mean for Jobs? The Future of Work." *Fortune*, March 15, 2017, pp. 22–24.

Argiro, Vincent. "Seeing in Volume." In *Pixel: The Magazine of Scientific Visualization* (July/ August 1990): 35–39.

Barter, Judith A. "Travels and Travails: Hopper's Late Pictures." In *Edward Hopper*. Boston, MA: MFA Publications, 2007.

Blinn, James. *Jim Blinn's Corner: Notation, Notation, Notation*. San Francisco, CA: Morgan Kaufman Publishers, 2003.

Bogen, J. E., and Bogen, G. M. "The Other Side of the Brain III: The Corpus Callosum and Creativity," *Bulletin of the Los Angeles Neurological Societies* 34 (1969): 191–220.

Boyle, Alix. "Beryl Benacerraf, MD" and "Richard Rogers, Architect," Yale Center for Dyslexia and Creativity, Yale School of Medicine, yale.dysexia.edu. Retrieved March 31, 2016.

Broecker, Wally. *The Great Ocean Conveyor: Discovering the Trigger for Abrupt Climate Change*. Princeton and Oxford: Princeton University Press, 2010.

Brown, D., H. Porta, and J. J. Uhl. "Calculus and *Mathematica*: A Laboratory Course for Learning by Doing," MAA Notes, 20 (1991): 99–110. In *The Laboratory Approach to Teaching Calculus*. Rev. ed. Edited by L. C. Leinbach, J. R. Hundhausen, A. M. Ostebee, L. J. Senechal, and D. B. Small. Washington, DC: Mathematical Association of America.

Burdett, Richard, ed. *Richard Rogers Partnership: Works and Projects*. New York: Monacelli, 1995.

California Institute of Technology. Oral History Project, sess. 1, tape 1, side 1. Interview of February 18, 1999, with Shirley K. Cohen. Published by Caltech Archives, 2005. Available as PDF at http://oralhistories.library .caltech.edu/108/.

Campbell, Lewis, and William Garnett. *The Life of James Clerk Maxwell, with a Selection from His Correspondence and Occasional Writings and a Sketch of His Contributions to Science*. Reprint, New York: Johnson Reprint, 1969. First published 1882 by MacMillan, London.

Card, Stuart K., Jock D. Mackinlay, and Ben Shneiderman, eds. *Readings in Information Visualization: Using Vision to Think*. San Francisco, CA: Morgan Kaufman Publishers, 1999.

———. *Readings in Information Visualization: Using Vision to Think*. San Francisco, CA: Morgan Kaufman, 2000.

Caroe, G. M. *William Henry Bragg: 1892–1942 Man and Scientist*. Cambridge: Cambridge University Press, 1978.

Channel Four Television. "Dyslexia." Three thirty-minute television programs produced by 20/20 for Channel Four Television. Broadcast in the United Kingdom, May 1999. Persons interviewed include Richard Branson, Sally Shaywitz, and Thomas West.

Davis, W., H. Porta, and J. Uhl. CALCULUS&*Mathematica*. Courseware including software and four texts. Reading, MA: Addison-Wesley, 1994.

Dowell, Ben. "Secret of the Super Successful . . . They're Dyslexic." *Sunday Times*, October 5, 2003, p. 1.

Dreyer, Janet Roman. Interview with the author. June 28, 2005.

Dreyer, William, Janet Dreyer, and Brandon King. Multiple conversations with the author. 2001–2004. Additional clarifications and further details were provided by Brandon King via e-mail, March 23, 2009.

Dukes, Helen, and Banesh Hoffmann. *Albert Einstein: The Human Side*. Princeton, NJ: Princeton University Press, 1979.

Dyslexia Association of Singapore. "Lee Kuan Yew, Singapore's Founding

Prime Minister, Visionary, Leader, Father and Builder of a Nation, 1923–2015." In *Embrace a Different Kind of Mind: Personal Stories of Dyslexia*, edited by Deborah Hewes, pp. 5–6. Singapore: Dyslexia Association of Singapore, 2015.

Dyslexia Foundation. "Talent & Dyslexia: Report of a 'Think Tank' Meeting, MIT Endicott House, April 26–27, 2003." Unpublished, undated draft report. Meeting planners and participants included Will Baker, Joyce Bulifant, Drake Duane, Jeff Gilger, Jerome Kagan, Peggy McArdle, Renee Merow, Phil Pasho, William F. Patterson, Charlotte Raymond, Glenn Rosen, Trey Roski, Daniel J. Sandin, Steve Schecter, Gordon F. Sherman, Delos R. Smith, Nicolas Smit, Catya von Károlyi, Thomas G. West, Ellen Winner, Maryanne Wolf and Frank Wood.

Economist. "Seeing Is Believing," August 19, 1995, p. 71.

Eide, Brock L., and Fernette F. Eide. *The Dyslexic Advantage: Unlocking the Hidden Potential of the Dyslexic Brain*. New York: Hudson Street, 2011.

Einstein, Albert. *Albert Einstein, the Human Side: New Glimpses from His Archives*. Selected and edited by Helen Dukas and Banesh Hoffmann. Princeton: Princeton University Press, 1979.

———. *Autobiographical Notes*. Translated and edited by Paul Arthur Schilpp (German and English on opposing pages). La Salle and Chicago, IL: Open Court, 1979. Originally published as vol. 7 of *The Library of Living Philosophers* (Evanston, IL), 1949.

———. *The Collected Papers of Albert Einstein*. Vol. 1. *The Early Years: 1879–1902*. Edited by John Stachel. (Documents in German, and other original languages, with introduction, commentary and notes in English.) Princeton, NJ: Princeton University Press, 1987.

———. "On the Electrodynamics of Moving Bodies." In *Einstein: A Centenary Volume*, edited by A. P. French. Cambridge, MA: Harvard University Press, 1979. Originally published 1905.

———. *Relativity: The Special and the General Theory*. Authorized translation by Robert W. Lawson. New York: Crown Publishers, 1961. Originally published 1916.

Everitt, C. W. F. "Maxwell's Scientific Creativity." In *Springs of Scientific Creativity: Essays on Founders of Modern Science*, edited by Rutherford Aris, H. Ted Davis, and Roger H. Stuewer. Minneapolis: University of Minnesota Press, 1983.

Faraday, Michael. *The Chemical History of a Candle*. New York: Harper and Brothers, Publishers, 1903.

———. *Experimental Researches in Electricity*. Vols. 1–3. Original publication by Taylor and Francis, 1839 and 1855. Reprint, New York: Dover, 1965.

Ferguson, Eugene S. *Engineering and the Mind's Eye*. Cambridge, MA: MIT Press, 1992.

Feynman, Richard P., Robert B. Leighton, and Matthew Sands. *The Feynman Lectures on Physics*. Reading, MA: Addison-Wesley, 1963.

Financial News. "Bringing the Gift of Sight to the Word Blind—Ben Thomson Is Chief Executive of the Noble Group, the Investment Banking Firm Based in Edinburgh. His Ruling Passion Is Dyslexia." Ruling Passions, *Financial News*, September 18, 2000.

Finke, Ronald A. *Principles of Mental Imagery*. Cambridge, MA: MIT Press, 1989.

French, A. P. "The Story of General Relativity." In *Einstein: A Centenary Volume*. Cambridge, MA: Harvard University Press, 1979.

Frey, Walter. "Schools Miss Out on Dyslexic Engineers." *IEEE Spectrum*. December 1990, p. 6.

Galaburda, Albert M., ed. *Dyslexia and Development: Neurobiological Aspects of Extra-Ordinary Brains*. Cambridge, MA: Harvard University Press, 1993.

Gardner, Howard. *Frames of Mind: The Theory of Multiple Intelligences*. New York: Basic Books, 1983.

———. *Intelligence Reframed: Multiple Intelligences for the 21st Century*. New York: Basic Books, Perseus Books, 1999.

Geschwind, Norman. "Biological Associations of Left-Handedness." *Annals of Dyslexia* 33 (1983): 29–40.

———. "The Brain of a Learning-Disabled Individual." *Annals of Dyslexia* 34 (1984): 319–27.

———. "Why Orton Was Right." *Annals of Dyslexia* 32. Orton Dyslexia Society Reprint no. 98 (1982).

Geschwind, Norman, and Albert Galaburda, eds. *Cerebral Dominance: The Biological Foundations*. Cambridge, MA: Harvard University Press, 1984.

———. "Cerebral Lateralization, Biological Mechanisms, Associations, and Pathology: A Hypothesis and a Program for Research, Parts I–III," *Archives of Neurology* 42 (May 1985): 428–59; (June 1985): 521–52; (July 1985): 634–54.

———. *Cerebral Lateralization: Biological Mechanisms, Associations, and Pathology*. Cambridge, MA: MIT Press, 1987.

Geschwind, Norman., and P. Behan. "Left-Handedness: Association with Immune Disease, Migraine, and Developmental Learning Disorder." *Proceedings of the National Academy of Sciences* 79 (1982): 5097–5100.

Geschwind, Norman, and W. Levitsky. "Human Brain: Left-Right Brain Asymmetries in Temporal Speech Region." *Science* 161 (1968): 186–87.

Gladwell, Malcolm. *David and Goliath: Underdogs, Misfits, and the Art of Battling Giants*. New York: Little, Brown, 2013.

Glazer, A. M., and Patience Thomson, eds. *Crystal Clear: The Autobiographies of Sir Lawrence and Lady Bragg*. Oxford, UK: Oxford University Press, 2015.

Gleick, James. *Chaos: Making a New Science*. New York: Viking, 1987.

———. *Genius: The Life and Science of Richard Feynman*. New York: Pantheon Books, 1992.

Gould, S. J. *Eight Little Piggies: Reflections in Natural History*. New York: W. W. Norton, 1993.

Grandin, Temple. *Thinking in Pictures: My Life with Autism*. With a foreword by Oliver Sacks. New York: Vintage Books, 2006. Originally published 1995.

Grandin, Temple, and Kate Duffy. *Developing Talents: Careers for Individuals with Asperger Syndrome and High Functioning Autism*. Foreword by Tony Atwood. Shawnee Mission, KS: Autism Asperger Publishing, 2004.

Grandin, Temple, and Richard Panek. *The Autistic Brain: Thinking Across the Spectrum*. New York: Houghton Mifflin Harcourt, 2013.

Grandin, Temple, and Sean Barron. *Unwritten Rules of Social Relationships: Decoding Social Mysteries through the Unique Perspectives of Autism.* Arlington, TX: Future Horizons, 2005.

Hadamard, J. *The Psychology of Invention in the Mathematical Field.* New York: Dover, 1954. Originally published 1945.

Hart C. E., L. Sharenbroich, B. J. Bornstein, D. Trout, B. King, E. Mjolsness, and B. J. Wold. "A Mathematical and Computational Framework for Quantitative Comparison and Integration of Large-Scale Gene Expression Data." *Nucleic Acids Research* 33, no. 8 (2005): 2580–94.

Haskell, Barbara, ed. *Georgia O'Keeffe: Abstraction.* New York: Whitney Museum of American Art and Yale University, 2009.

Hetland, Lois, Ellen Winner, Shirley Veenema, and Kimberley M. Sheridan. *Studio Thinking: The Real benefits of Visual Arts Education.* Teachers College, Columbia University. New York: Teachers College Press, 2007.

Hoffman, Banesh. *Albert Einstein: Creator and Rebel.* New York: New American Library, 1972.

Holton, G. "On Trying to Understand Scientific Genius." *American Scholar* 41 (1972): 95–110.

Horner, Jack [John R.], and James Gorman. *How to Build a Dinosaur (The New Science of Reverse Evolution).* New York: Plume, Penguin Group, 2009.

Horner, John ("Jack"). Videotaped discussion with Thomas G. West, filmed by NHK cameraman (Tokyo, Japan) on site of dinosaur dig, far northern central Montana on the Canadian border, about nine minutes long, July 5, 2007. Personal collection of Thomas G. West. NHK DVD, not broadcast.

Horner, John R., and Edwin Dobb. *Dinosaur Lives: Unearthing an Evolutionary Saga.* New York: HarperCollins, 1997.

Hussin, Aziz. "S[enior] M[inister] Donates Royalties to Dyslexia Body." *Straits Times* (Singapore), January 18, 1996, p. 3.

Huxley, Aldous. *Brave New World.* London: Vintage Classics, Random House. Cover design, detail from *City in Shards of Light* by Carolyn Hubbard-Ford, Private Collection / Bridgeman Art Library, 1932, reissued 2004.

Jolls, K. R., and Coy, D.C. "The Art of Thermodynamics." *IRIS Universe: The Magazine of Visual Processing* 12 (1990): 31–36.

Jones, Bence. *The Life and Letters of Faraday*. Vols. 1, 2. Philadelphia: J. B. Lippincott, 1870.

Kahney, Leander. *Jony Ive: The Genius behind Apple's Greatest Products*. New York: Penguin, 2013.

Kaufmann, William J., and Larry L. Smarr. *Supercomputing and the Transformation of Science*. New York: Scientific American Library, 1993.

Kawaharada, Dennis. "Wayfinding, or Non-Instrument Navigation," Polynesian Voyaging Society, May 2002, http://leahi.kcc.Hawaii.edu/org/pvs/. (The *Hokule'a* has been sailing around the world since May 2014—and in January 2017 it had traveled through the Panama Canal and was in the Pacific Ocean once again, on its way home. See: The Polynesian Voyaging Society, www.hokulea.com, and related websites.)

Kilham, Benjamin. *Out on a Limb: What Black Bears Have Taught Me about Intelligence and Intuition*. White River Junction, VT: Chelsea Green Publishing, 2013.

King, Brandon. E-mail clarifications about data visualization and help for a PhD student and his professor. Addressed to Thomas G. West. March 23, 2009.

Kolata, Gina. "Computer Graphics Comes to Statistics." *Science* 217 (September 3, 1982): 919–20.

Kupfer, Andrew. "Craig McCaw Sees an Internet in the Sky." *Fortune*, May 27, 1996, p. 64ff.

Levy, Steven. *In the Plex: How Google Thinks, Works, and Shapes Our Lives*. New York: Simon and Schuster, 2011.

Lewis, Michael. *The Big Short: Inside the Doomsday Machine*. New York: W. W. Norton, 2010.

Lovelock, James. "Daisy World: A Cybernetic Proof of the Gaia Hypothesis." *CoEvolution Quarterly* 38. Sausalito, CA: Point, June 21, 1983.

———. Foreword to *The Rough Guide to Climate Change: The Symptoms, the Science, the Solutions* by Robert Henson. 3rd ed. London: Rough Guides, 2006.

———. *The Revenge of Gaia: Why the Earth Is Fighting Back—and How We Can Still Save Humanity*. London: Allen Lane, Penguin Books, 2006.

Low, Sam. *Hawaiki Rising: Hokule'a Nainoa Thompson, and the Hawaiian Renaissance*. Waipahu, HI: Island Heritage Publishing, 2013.

Lucangeli, Daniela (conference chair). *International Academy for Research in Learning Disabilities, 36th Annual Conference*. IARLD and Universita Degli Studi Di Padova, Padua, Italy, Palazzo del Bo, June 7–9, 2012. Edizioni Erickson, Via del Pioppeto 24, 38121 Trento, Italy.

Ma, Kwan-Lui. "Visualization: A Quickly Emerging Field." *Computer Graphics* 38, no. 1 (Feb. 2004): 4–7.

Mail Online. "Dyslexia Is Britain's Secret Weapon in the Spy War." July 13, 2013. http://www.dailymail.co.uk/news/article-2362793/Dyslexia -Britains-secret-weapon-spy-war-Top-codebreakers-crack-complex -problems-suffer-condition.html.

Makri, Anita. Review of *Climate Change and the Health of Nations: Famines, Fevers, and the Fate of Populations* by McMichael, Anthony J. Oxford, UK: Oxford University Press, 2017. "Back to the Future: An Epidemiologist Takes a Long View of Our Fraught Relationship with the Environment." *Science* 355, no. 6323 (January 27, 2017): 355.

Mandelbrot, Benoit B. *The Fractal Geometry of Nature*. Updated and augmented ed. New York: W. H. Freeman, 1983. Originally published 1977.

McCalman, Iain. *Darwin's Armada: Four Voyages and the Battle for the Theory of Evolution*. New York: W. W. Norton, 2009.

McDonald, Kim A., "The Iconoclastic Fossil Hunter." *Chronicle of Higher Education*, November 16, 1994, A9–A17.

More, Mark A. "Historic Bath: Edna Ferber and the James Adams Floating Theater." North Carolina History, www.nchistoricsites.org/bath/edna-ferber.htm. Retrieved March 2017.

Morgan, W. Pringle. "A Case of Congenital Word-Blindness." *British Medical Journal*, November 7, 1896, p. 1378.

Morowitz, Harold J., and Eric Smith. *The Origin and Nature of Life on Earth:*

The Emergence of the Fourth Geosphere. Cambridge, UK: Cambridge University Press, 2016.

Morris, Betsy. "The Dyslexic CEO: Charles Schwab, Richard Branson, Craig McCaw & John Chambers Triumphed over America's No.1 Learning Disorder. Your Kid Can Too." *Fortune*, May 20, 2002.

———. "What a Life." Special issue, *Fortune: The Business Life Issue*, October 6, 2003, pp. 50–60.

Negroponte, Nicholas. *Being Digital.* New York: Alfred A. Knopf, 1995.

Nicolson, Roderick I. *Positive Dyslexia.* Sheffield, UK: Rodin Books, 2015.

Nicolson, Roderick I., and Angela Fawcett. *Dyslexia, Learning and the Brain.* Cambridge, MA: MIT Press, 2008.

Norman, Donald A. *Things That Make Us Smart: Defending Human Attributes in an Age of the Machine.* Reading, MA: Addison-Wesley, 1993.

O'Connell, Kenneth R., Vincent Argiro, John Andrew Berton Jr., Craig Hickman, and Thomas G. West. "Visual Thinkers in an Age of Computer Visualization," *Computer Graphics: The Proceedings of the Annual Conference of ACM SIGGRAPH*, August 1993, pp. 379–80.

O'Neill, Helen. *Life without Limits: The Remarkable Story of David Pescud and His Fight for Survival in a Sea of Words.* Auckland, NZ: Random House New Zealand, 2003.

Pais, Abraham. *"Subtle Is the Lord . . .": The Science and the Life of Albert Einstein.* Oxford: Oxford University Press, 1982.

Park, Kyungmee. *A Comparative Study of the Traditional Calculus Course vs. the CALCULUS&Mathematica Course.* Unpublished PhD thesis, Graduate School of Education, University of Illinois at Urbana–Champaign, dated September 1992, transmittal letter December 5, 1993.

Parker, Ian. "The Shape of Things to Come: How an Industrial Designer Became Apple's Greatest Product." *New Yorker*, March 2, 2015, pp. 120–39.

Parloff, Roger. "Deep Learning Revolution," *Fortune*, October 2016, pp. 96–106.

Patterson, Scott. *The Quants: How a New Breed of Math Whizzes Conquered Wall Street and Nearly Destroyed It.* New York: Crown Publishing, 2010.

Pearson, E. S. *Karl Pearson: An Appreciation of Some Aspects of His Life and Work*. Cambridge: University Press, 1938.

———. "Some Aspects of the Geometry of Statistics: The Use of Visual Presentation in Understanding the Theory and Application of Mathematical Statistics." In *The Selected Papers of E.S. Pearson*. Presented as the Inaugural Address of the President to the Royal Statistical Society in 1956. Barclay and Los Angeles: University of California Press, 1966.

Pearson, Karl. *The Life, Letters and Labours of Francis Galton*. Vol. 1. *Birth 1822 to Marriage 1853*. Cambridge, UK: Cambridge University Press, 1914.

Perry, Rachael Berenson. "Indiana Realities: Regional Paintings 1930–1945." *American Art Review* 23, no. 2 (March–April 2011): 68–75.

Petzinger, Thomas. "A Banc One Executive Credits His Success to Mastering Dyslexia," Front Lines, *Wall Street Journal*, April 24, 1998, p. B1.

Reid, Gavin. *Dyslexia: A Complete Guide for Parents and Those Who Help Them*. 2nd ed. New York: Wiley-Blackwell, 2011.

Reid, Gavin, and Jane Kirk. *Dyslexia in Adults: Education and Employment*. New York: John Wiley and Sons, 2001.

Reiff, Henry B., and Nicole S. Ofiesh. *Teaching for the Lifespan: Successfully Transitioning Students with Learning Disabilities to Adulthood*. Foreword by Thomas G. West. Thousand Oaks, CA, and London: SAGE Publications, 2016.

Ritchie-Calder, P. *Leonardo & the Age of the Eye*. New York: Simon and Schuster, 1970.

Robins, Cynthia. "One Man's Battle against Dyslexia—How Financier Charles Schwab Is Helping Others Whose Kids Have Learning Disabilities." *San Francisco Examiner*, March 8, 1992, pp. D3, D10.

Robison, John Elder. *Be Different: My Adventures with Asperger's and My Advice for Fellow Aspergians, Misfits, Families, and Teachers*. New York: Broadway Paperbacks, Crown, Random House, 2011.

———. *Look Me in the Eye: My Life with Asperger's*. New York: Three Rivers, 2008. Originally published 2007.

———. *Raising Cubby: A Father and Son's Adventures with Asperger's, Trains, Tractors and High Explosives*. New York: Crown Publishers, 2013.

———. *Switched On: A Memoir of Brain Change and Emotional Awakening*. With a foreword by Alvaro Pascual-Leone. New York: Spiegel and Grau, Penguin Random House, 2016.

Roccaforte, Marianne. *Bridges in the Mind: An Artist's Handbook for Everyday Living*. Hopkins, MN: Benu, 2010.

Roden J. C., B. W. King, D. Trout, A. Mortazavi, B. J. Wold, and C. E. Hart. "Mining Gene Expression Data by Interpreting Principal Components." *BMC Bioinformatics* 7 (2006): 194.

Sacks, Oliver. *An Anthropologist on Mars: Seven Paradoxical Tales*. New York: Alfred A. Knopf, 1995.

———. *The Mind's Eye*. New York: Alfred A. Knopf, 2010.

Sahlberg, Pasi. *Finnish Lessons: What Can the World Learn from Educational Change in Finland?* New York: Teachers College Press, Columbia University, 2010.

Satori, G. "Leonardo Da Vinci, Omo Sanza Lettere: A Case of Surface Dysgraphia?" *Cognitive Neuropsychology* 4, no. 1 (1987): 1–10.

Schneps, Matthew. Harvard-Smithsonian Center for Astro-Physics. Laboratory for Visual Learning, 2013 (site discontinued).

Schneps, Matthew H., James R. Brockmole, Gerhard Sonnert, and Marc Pomplun. "History of Reading Struggles Linked to Enhanced Learning in Low Spatial Frequency Scenes." *PLoS One* 7, no. 4 (2012): e35724, www.plosone.org, open access, freely available online. Short reference: "Dyslexia Linked to Strengths for Scene Memory."

Schultz, Philip. *My Dyslexia*. New York: W. W. Norton, 2011.

Scurfield, Matthew. *I Could Be Anyone*. Gharb, Gozo, Malta: Monticello, 2008.

Seligman, M. E. P. *Learned Optimism*. New York: Knopf, 1990.

Sellin, David. *Francis Speight: A Retrospective, November 7–December 6, 1986*. Washington, DC: Taggard, Jorgensen, and Putman, 1986.

Shlain, Leonard. *The Alphabet versus the Goddess: The Conflict between Word and Image*. New York: Viking, 1998.

Snow, C. P. "Albert Einstein, 1879–1955." In *Einstein: A Centenary Volume*, edited by A. P. French. Cambridge, MA: Harvard University Press, 1979.

Steen, Lynn Arthur. "Mathematics Education: A Predictor of Scientific Competitiveness." *Science* 237 (1987): 251–52, 302.

———, ed. *Heading the Call for Change: Suggestions for Curricular Action*. Washington, DC: Mathematical Association of America, 1992.

———. "The Science of Patterns." *Science* 240 (1988): 611–16.

Strand, Mark. *Hopper*. New York: Alfred A. Knopf, 2011. Originally published 1994.

Tauber, Alfred I., and Scott H. Podolsky. *The Generation of Diversity: Clonal Selection Theory and the Rise of Molecular Immunology*. Cambridge, MA: Harvard University Press, 1997.

Thompson, D'Arcy Wentworth. *On Growth and Form*. Vols. 1 and 2. 2nd ed. Cambridge: Cambridge University Press, 1942. Reprinted in the Netherlands by Ysel Press, Deventer, 1972.

Thompson, Nainoa. "Voyage into the New Millennium." *Hana Hou!* February/March 2000, pp. 41 ff.

Thomson, Alice. *The Singing Line: The Story of the Man Who Strung the Telegraph across Australia, and the Woman Who Gave Her Name to Alice Springs*. London: Chatto and Windus, 1999.

Thomson, Hugh. *The White Rock: An Exploration of the Inca Heartland*. New York: Overlook , Peter Mayer Publishers, 2003. Originally published 2001.

Tolstoy, Ivan. *James Clerk Maxwell: A Biography*. Chicago: University of Chicago Press, 1981.

Turner, Elizabeth Hutton. *Georgia O'Keeffe: The Poetry of Things*. Washington, DC: Phillips Collection, 1999. Published on the occasion of the exhibitions in 1999–2000 at museums in Washington, DC; Dallas, TX; San Francisco, CA; and Santa Fe, MN.

Tyndall, John. *Faraday as a Discoverer*. London: Longmans, Green, 1868.

von Károlyi, Catya. "Visual-Spatial Strength in Dyslexia: Rapid Discrimination of Impossible Figures." *Journal of Learning Disabilities* 34, no. 4 (July/August 2001): 380–91.

von Károlyi, Catya, and Ellen Winner. "Dyslexia and Visual Spatial Talents: Are They Connected?" In *Students with Both Gifts and Learning Disabilities*, edited by R. J. Sternberg and T. Newman. New York: Springer-Verlag, 2003.

von Károlyi, Catya, Ellen Winner, Wendy Gray, and Gordon Sherman. "Dyslexia Linked to Talent: Global Visual-Spatial Ability." *Brain and Language*, May 2003.

Wardens, Cotswold, and the Ramblers Association. *Country Walks around Blockley*. Gloucester, UK: Gloucester County Council, Shire Hall, 1991.

Watson, James D. *The Double Helix: A Personal Account of the Discovery of DNA*. With a foreword by Sir Lawrence Bragg. New York: Atheneum, 1968.

Weiner, Norbert. *Cybernetics: Or Control and Communication in the Animal and the Machine*. Cambridge, MA: MIT Press, 1996. Originally published 1948.

———. *The Human Use of Human Beings: Cybernetics and Society*. New York: Avon Books, Hearst, 1954. Originally published 1950.

West, Thomas G. "The Abilities of Those with Reading Disabilities: Focusing on the Talents of People with Dyslexia." Chap. 11 in *Reading and Attention Disorders: Neurobiological Correlates*, edited by Drake D. Duane. Baltimore, MD: York, 1999.

———. "Amazing Shortcomings, Amazing Strengths: Beginning to Understand the Hidden Talents of Dyslexics." *Asia Pacific Journal of Developmental Differences* 1, no. 1 (January 2014): 78–89. (A publication of the Dyslexia Association of Singapore [DAS].)

———. "Brain Drain, Reconsidering Spatial Ability." Images and Reversals, *Computer Graphics*, August 1998, pp. 15.

———. Foreword to *Forgotten Letters: An Anthology of Literature by Dyslexic Writers*, edited by Naomi Folb. London: RASP, 2011.

———. "Forward into the Past: A Revival of Old Visual Talents with Computer Visualization." *Computer Graphics* 29, no. 4, edited by Karen Sullivan, November 1995, pp. 14–19.

———. "A Future of Reversals: Dyslexic Talents in a World of Computer Visualization." *Annals of Dyslexia* 42 (1992): 124–39.

———. "The Gifts of Dyslexia: Talents among Dyslexics and Their Families." *Hong Kong Journal of Paediatrics (New Series)* 10 (2005): 153–58.

———. "Left Behind in the Beginning of the Race: The Paradoxes of Dyslexia." In *Embrace a Different Kind of Mind: Personal Stories of Dyslexia*, edited by Deborah Hewes, pp. xxiii–xxviii. Singapore: Dyslexia Association of Singapore, 2015.

———. *In the Mind's Eye: Visual Thinkers, Gifted People with Learning Difficulties, Computer Images, and the Ironies of Creativity*. 1st ed. Buffalo, NY: Prometheus Books, 1991.

———. *In the Mind's Eye: Visual Thinkers, Gifted People with Dyslexia and Other Learning Difficulties, Computer Images, and the Ironies of Creativity*. Updated ed. with a new preface and epilogue. Amherst, NY: Prometheus Books, 1997.

———. *In the Mind's Eye: Creative Visual Thinkers, Gifted Dyslexics and the Rise of Visual Technologies*. 2nd ed. With a foreword by Oliver Sacks. Amherst, NY: Prometheus Books, 2009.

———. "A Return to Visual Thinking." *Computer Graphics World*, November 1992.

———. "A Return to Visual Thinking." In *Proceedings, Science and Scientific Computing: Visions of a Creative Symbiosis. Symposium of Computer Users in the Max Planck Gesellschaft*, edited and translated by P. Wittenburg and T. Plesser. Göttingen, Germany, November 1993 (published 1994). (Paper published in German: Rückkehr zum visuellen Denken, Forschung und wissenschftliches Rechnen: Beiträge anläßlich des 10. EDV-Benutzertreffens der Max-Planck-Gesellschaft in Göttingen, November 1993.)

———. "Medieval Clerk to Renaissance Thinker: Design, Visualization and Technological Change." Presentation published on CD-ROM documenting the proceedings of the first Doors of Perception conference, Stedelijk Museum, Amsterdam, Holland, October 30–31, 1993. Published in Amsterdam as part of *Mediamatic* 8, no. 1 (September 1994).

———. "Playing with Images: A Return to Thinking in Pictures." *Computers in*

Physics 10, no. 5, edited by Lewis M. Holmes (Sept./Oct. 1996): 413. (A publication of the American Institute of Physics.)

———. "Summary, National Library of Medicine Visualization Research Agenda Meeting: The Impact of Visualization Technologies—Using Vision to Think." February 15–16, 2000.

———. *Thinking like Einstein: Returning to Our Visual Roots with the Emerging Revolution in Computer Information Visualization.* Amherst, NY: Prometheus Books, 2004.

———. "Upside Down: Visual-Spatial Talents and Technological Change." *Understanding Our Gifted* 8, no. 3 (Jan./Feb. 1996): 1–11.

———. "Visualization in the Mind's Eye." *IRIS Universe: The Magazine of Visual Processing*, no. 14, November 1990.

———. "Visual Thinkers and Nobel Prizes." Images and Reversals, *Computer Graphics*, February 2001. Based on the conference Genius in the Genes? held at Green College, Oxford University, Oxford, UK, November 18, 2000.

———. "Visual Thinkers, Mental Models and Computer Visualization." In *Interactive Learning through Visualization: The Impact of Computer Graphics in Education*, edited by Steve Cunningham and Roger J. Hubbold. Berlin and Heidelberg: Springer-Verlag, 1992.

Winner, Ellen. *Gifted Children: Myths and Realities.* New York: Basic Books, 1996.

Winner, Ellen, Catya von Károlyi, and Daphna Malinsky. "Dyslexia and Visual-Spatial Talents: No Clear Link." *Perspectives* (Spring 2000): 27–30.

Winner, Ellen, Catya von Károlyi, Daphna Malinsky, Lisa French, Colleen Seliger, Erin Ross, and Christina Weber. "Dyslexia and Visual-Spatial Talents: Compensation vs. Deficit Model." *Brain and Language* 76 (2001): 81–110.

Witt-Miller, Harriet. "The Soft, Warm, Wet Technology of Native Oceania." *Whole Earth Review* (Fall 1991): 64–69.

Wolf, Maryanne. *Dyslexia, Fluency, and the Brain.* Baltimore, MD: York, 2001.

Yeo, Geraldine. "Dyslexia: S[enior M[inister]'s Case Gives Parents Hope—

They Are Motivated, Encouraged by His Example." *Straits Times* (Singapore), January 19, 1996, p. 25.

Zimmerman, Walter, and Steven Cunningham. *Visualization in Teaching and Learning Mathematics*. Washington, DC: Mathematical Association of America, 1991.

INDEX